Play Works

Helping Children Learn through Play

SUSANNE T. EDEN

authorHOUSE®

AuthorHouse™
1663 Liberty Drive, Suite 200
Bloomington, IN 47403
www.authorhouse.com
Phone: 1-800-839-8640

First published by AuthorHouse 7/16/2008

ISBN: 978-1-4343-6519-4 (sc)

Library of Congress Control Number: 2008905431

Printed in the United States of America
Bloomington, Indiana

This book is printed on acid-free paper.

To Wilf:

Remember a puppet named Archie?

To my beloved Norfolk terriers:

    Maggie, who was there at the beginning, and

    Molly, who is here at the end.

And to all the children who have shared their play with me.

Table of Contents

Part 4
Resources and References

Preface

Over the past decade, there has been a worldwide awakening to the fact that the early years matter. We have known for a long time that the first years of life are important. This is not new. But what has changed is that today's interest is driven by both biological and economic factors. Biological research has firmly established that by age six, a child's behavior and capacity to learn are set. Recognition that the long-term economic future of a society rests upon how well our children thrive in these first years of life has further sparked a global response to better provide for the health and education of young children.

In the many projects that have been initiated, while all agree that better beginnings for children will result in stronger, healthier societies, there is little mention of play. If anything, play has receded further into the background of childhood than it was a decade ago. Yet there is substantial research to support the claim that play is the way children learn that which no one could teach them.

Play works as the foremost means of development and learning in the early years. In writing this book, I hope that parents, teachers of young children, and caregivers will gain understanding of what play is, how children play, what they are learning, and what we can do to help. By understanding the workings of play, we will gain a new respect for the power of play and the right of every child to have the time, space and means of growing through play.

Providing the best for our children requires a partnership between home, preschool, and school as well as with the various caregivers entrusted with young children. Whether parent, caregiver, or teacher, we all need to be singing from the same page. A harmonious relationship built on mutual trust and respect will go a long way toward ensuring the best beginning for every child.

Over my career I have been involved with education at all levels, and there is no doubt in my mind that pouring money into secondary and post-secondary education to the neglect of the early years is simply foolish.

My hope in writing this book is that it will confirm what parents see every day as the miracle of learning through play, that it will empower the many dedicated teachers and caregivers to stand firm in their belief in the power of play, and, finally, that it will result in restoring play to children both at home and in schools.

Acknowledgments

A book is never one person's story. It represents the coming together of experiences and ideas drawn from many contacts, both direct and indirect. I wish to acknowledge the many dedicated professionals whose studies of play provided a platform for my own inquiry. Their scholarship has enriched me immeasurably.

I also wish to acknowledge the many people, both children and adults, who have had a part in my journey toward understanding play. It would not have been possible to request permission from all those whose stories appear in this book, so I have changed the names and in some cases the context to protect their identities. To all of the children who let me into their play, the teachers who let me into their classrooms, and the parents who let me into their homes, I offer my sincerest appreciation.

Finally, I wish to honor the memory of four educators who are no longer here to receive my thanks:

> *Dr Otto Weininger and Richard Courtney, professors, Ontario Institute for Studies in Education*
>
> *Patricia Cooper and Brenda Grandinetti, kindergarten teachers without parallel*

I also wish to thank Laura Mae Lindo, my research assistant, for her invaluable contribution. Meeting her at this juncture was indeed a bonus.

I appreciate the interest and assistance of the AuthorHouse staff who have guided me through the process of publishing this book.

Photographs

Many of the photographs in this book are my own, but I wish to thank Anita Lariviere for contributing the following photos on pages 5, 62, 66, 159, 222. Her generosity in sharing these pictures is much appreciated. I also wish to thank Ruth Magnusdottir for photos on pages 18 and 167.

Back cover by Robert G. Ward

*Play is the finest system of education
known to mankind.*

Neville Scarfe,
Dean Emeritus,
University of British Columbia

Part 1

Play: What's Going On?

Play is the highest expression of human development in childhood for it alone is the free expression of what is in the soul.

Frederich Froebel

Introduction

How many times as a parent or teacher have you found yourself saying, "There's too much noise in there. What's going on?"

"We're just playing," comes the reply.

"Well play quietly!"

This familiar scene happens over and over at home and school. We may tolerate play but rarely do we celebrate it. To a large degree this is because we do not understand play, nor do we see the importance of play to every aspect of our child's development. Anything as noisy and as much fun as play cannot be good, or so we may think. Yet if we understood play and its importance to human development, we would become more tolerant and return play to its place as the premier way children learn that which no one could teach them.

Even when we try to understand what is happening, it is often difficult for us to interpret what the children are doing.

Evelyn has come this morning as a parent volunteer to assist in her daughter Taylor's junior kindergarten classroom. When she arrives, she finds the children at play. A confusing number of activities are going on all at the same time.

Evelyn watches the kaleidoscope of motion flowing in and around the home center. Children move in and out, coming together in twos and threes, sometimes playing alone, and coming back with new partners. The roles they play seem to change without explanation so that she is not sure who is mother, who the father. As Evelyn watches, she is quick to find fault with the logic of what the children say and do. "I'm not your husband," Andy exclaims, "I'm the daddy." Bare-naked babies do not get washed in the same pan as the dishes!

3

As the play continues, Evelyn is struck by how absorbed the children are. Nothing distracts them from their make-believe play. So realistic are their actions as they wash the dishes that Evelyn almost believes that there is water in the basin. She begins to see that a story is unfolding. It is a story from everyday life, but with a difference. As she listens, she hears dialogue spoken in the tone of voice and style of an exasperated parent. She recognizes herself when she overhears her daughter say, "These damn kids are driving me crazy. You look after them, I'm going shopping." Uncomfortable with the mirror image the play provides, Evelyn moves away to help a child with a craft activity.

In speaking afterward with me, Evelyn confided that her husband had been in New York on business and on return announced that he needed to relax and was off to play squash with a friend. Needless to say, Evelyn, who had been home for nearly a week with three children under the age of five, was not happy. It was a revelation that her young daughter could capture her mood and attitude so precisely.

What is a parent to make of all this confusion called play? What are the children doing that has anything to do with school? Where is the quiet controlled classroom she remembers from her childhood? Where is the teacher?

The teacher may be involved with an individual child or a small group in another part of the room. She may be in the midst of the play wearing a hat and sipping coffee at the pretend party. She may be standing apart, unobtrusively observing and learning about the children from their play.

Like the parent, the teacher too has many questions about play. Should I get involved or remain apart? Should I redirect these children who play here day after day? What can I do to help the onlooker who is not accepted by the others? Is it getting too noisy? Too messy? How can I justify play in terms of my curriculum plans? How can I convince parents and school officials that play is important for all children, not just the slower ones?

The answers to these questions all begin with understanding why play is important and the nature of children's play. Once we grasp how play works, we can better understand why play is the way children learn and how to support learning through play without interfering.

1
Why Play?

We are born to play. Children play purposefully, as we can see by watching the dedication they bring to a game. "The difference between smart people and brilliant people," one visionary remarked, "is that brilliant people know how to play."

M. Ferguson and M. Kellner-Rogers

The play of children is a joyous manifestation of mankind at its best. It captures the curiosity, wonder, and magic of our remarkable world. Play, as the term is used in this book, is understood to be both a social activity and a psychological process. Play is self-directed pretending. It actively engages both the body and the mind and is free from imposed rules. Play is play. It is not playing something as we often use the term for such things as playing golf or playing the violin. Play is learning.

So important is play for the young child that in 1948, the United Nations declared play an essential right of all children. More recently this right was reaffirmed in Article 31 of the *United Nations Convention on the Rights of the Child*, adopted by the UN General Assembly in November 1989. This article states that every child has a right to leisure, play, and participation in cultural and artistic activities.

For Further Information see Commentary on the United Nations Convention on the Rights of the Child, Article 31 by David Paulo, 2006

What Makes Play Important?

What would prompt a serious organization dealing with the most challenging situations on the planet to devote time to forging a resolution on children's play? Play is an essential activity of childhood, as important for growth and development as food and shelter. It is through play that children learn about themselves and the world around them. Healthy children around the globe play with absorption and spontaneity. There is no other activity that can compare with play as a means of healthy development and learning.

Play influences all aspects of development. Without play, the development of the mind, body, and spirit is stunted. Without play, a child can never enjoy the gift of friendship, for it is in play that children first experience the give-and-take that makes up true and lasting friendships. Without play, children would never know what it is to create, to sing, to dance and twirl with abandon.

For nearly fifty years, children's play and its role in early learning has been a hot topic of research in all fields of the social sciences. Anthropologists, psychologists, and sociologists, as well as educators, have explored many dimensions of play and learning. This explosion of research confirms the powerful effect play has on virtually every aspect of human development and learning.

Recent interest in play and learning builds on a solid historic tradition. One of the best known of the early champions of play is Fredrick Froebel (1898), who believed that play was the highest form of human activity in childhood. Froebel is considered to be the father of modern kindergarten, and his influence can be seen even today in the selection of many of the toys and the arrangement of the learning environment in preschools and kindergartens. Although Froebel's vision of education belongs to another time and place, the key principles of his theory continue to influence beliefs about early education.

During the last century, the work of the Swiss scholar Jean Piaget (1969) further contributed to understanding how children learn and the importance of play in the early years.

Along with Jean Piaget, the work of Lev Vygotsky (1962, 1976), a Russian developmental psychologist, has had a profound influence on our understandings of child development and the importance of play.

Vygotsky recognized that all play involves the use of imagination and believed that play is the most important activity of childhood in terms of learning. Vygotsky stressed the role of social interaction as experienced in play as a crucial ingredient to learning through play. While earlier researchers thought of the play of infants and toddlers as "solitary," Vygotsky recognized the importance of social interaction right from the earliest stage.

Playing with others leads to learning how to work together and live together in harmony. All around the globe we see hatred and violence erupting, pitting one group against another at great cost, both human and economic. We read accounts of our own children perpetrating acts of extreme violence against other children. Physically violent and antisocial behavior does not begin in adolescence. It has its roots in the early years. It has been reported that children as young as eighteen months have resorted to physical violence excessively. In one longitudinal study during the mid-1980s, children who exhibited serious violent and antisocial behavior in junior kindergarten were followed for four years in regular classrooms. A variety of intervention strategies were used to try to change the behaviors, and the teachers were provided with support. At the end of the study, the conclusion was that children who were physically violent at age four got progressively more so each year, even with intervention. There was no evidence of a turnaround for any of these children.

More recently, Tremblay, Haapasalo and Masse (1994), of the Canadian Institute for Advanced Research (CIFAR), found similar results. In their longitudinal study of antisocial behavior in children, Tremblay and his colleagues tracked children from school entry to adulthood. They found that antisocial behavior in adolescents and adults could be traced back to behavioral problems on school entry. Tremblay examines a number of factors in his research, focusing on parental practices as key to the origins of antisocial behavior.

> For information on this study and related research see www.cifar.ca.

For young children, conflict is primarily about issues of power. Babies are born helpless and spend their early years seeking to overcome the feeling of being powerless. As children gain power over one aspect or another of their lives, self-confidence begins to emerge. Children need to feel that they control some things in their lives. This may be as basic as control over their walking or eating. In later childhood, control extends to more important aspects, such as choosing friends, clothing, and so on.

Power is at the heart of relationships. During the first years, most play relationships are what might be called dominant-submissive, that is, one person is the boss and the other does what she is told. By school age, children have begun to form friendships based on reciprocal power. In this relationship both parties are equal, although I have observed that young children often engage in friendships with those who are more mature and therefore have more power, or with those who are less mature and can be bossed about.

Play and Education

Many studies have examined the links between play and educational goals. Sara Smilansky (1990), in her landmark studies of the sociodramatic play of children in Israel, found connections between pretend play and readiness for reading and for mathematics. She found those children who were superior players were best able to "play the school game." In other words, they were better prepared for the demands of traditional schooling.

One of the most compelling arguments for play is its role in the development of creativity and imagination. Among those who have studied this aspect of play and learning, none has contributed more than Dorothy and Jerome Singer (1992, 2000). As early as the 1970s, they championed the power of play to develop creativity and imagination. Their more recent work, published in 2001, has examined how pretend play helps prepare children for school success. In their work, they emphasize the importance of adults as full play partners. In their studies they found that learning was more in evidence when the parent or caregiver was actively and playfully involved.

A program based on play is truly a program for the gifted. It has been shown that it is the most able children who choose to engage in sociodramatic play. When teachers of young children try to justify a play-based program, parents will sometimes come back with—as a parent once snapped at me—"That's all well and good, but it won't get him into the right university when the time comes." This is nonsense. Leaders are those who can imagine new ways of doing things. Success in higher education will depend more on the ability to think outside the box than it will on the ability to memorize and regurgitate what has been taught.

Another strand that threads its way through the discussion of play and learning is that of cultural diversity. There are certainly universal aspects of play that have been found across many cultures. These include such things as play with dolls, play fighting, physical play, and even some games with rules, modified to reflect the specific culture.

Play is a valuable resource for promoting equality and cultural awareness among young children. They tend to take people on face value and ignore differences of race and, until school age, gender. Through play, children learn about their own culture and that of those who are different. In today's shrinking world this is becoming increasingly important. Many classrooms have children of vastly different cultural backgrounds. Through playing together, children learn that different is a positive thing and that there is no need to fear the unfamiliar.

Play is a means of exploring cultural value. The issue of competition, for example, is treated differently in different cultures. While North American children tend to be steeped in competition, aboriginal people from different cultures value sharing rather than competing. When these children come together in play, the children can learn many lessons from one another. Play has room for these kinds of cultural differences, allowing children to work out their own cultural behaviors as well as understand those of other cultures.

The content of play will reflect the experiences the individual children have. This was brought home to me during a visit to northern

Labrador. The children in the urban community in which I live will choose to play going to restaurants, driving the car, and being cared for by babysitters, among other things. The children I played with in the northern school were going trapping on their snowmobiles. Babysitting was unfamiliar to them. In their community, families look after one another.

There are many studies that examine the links between play and the development of literacy, that is, reading and writing. Play offers a powerful motivation to learn how to talk and listen as a means of joining in with others.

The whole point with play is that it offers a complete package. It does not merely contribute to one aspect or another of development, but addresses the whole child in all her developmental needs—physical, intellectual, social, and emotional. As research shows, there is no aspect of the child's life that cannot be enriched by play. In fact, there are many aspects of healthy development that cannot be addressed any other way. We erode play at the risk of eroding healthy development in our children.

Challenges to Play

For all of the serious attention given to children's play in the past, play seems to hold little value in today's society. A phenomenon referred to as the *disappearance of childhood* highlights the erosion of the play life of our young children. Whether in the home, the preschool, or school, play is often looked upon as a waste of time, or at best, a needed diversion between the important lessons of the traditional curriculum. I've heard parents complain that in a particular preschool the children do nothing but play. I've heard many a complaint that junior kindergartens rich in play experiences are nothing more than a babysitting service. These comments reflect an attitude of disregard for children and their play. This attitude comes from those who believe that children cannot be free to play lest, as Chilton-Pearce said so many years ago in his book *The Magical Child* (1977), they grow up "as tares in a field, wild and uncontrollable."

A major challenge to play in education is what has become known as the *pushed-down curriculum*. In both the United States and Canada, children are eligible to enter kindergarten according to an arbitrary date on a calendar that can vary widely from jurisdiction to jurisdiction. In regions that offer junior kindergarten programs, children who are four by the end of December are able to enter school. In other regions, children who are five by the end of December enter senior kindergarten. The dates vary, but there is a full year's difference in age between one child and another in the same class. When we consider that to a four-year-old this represents a quarter of his life experience, the difference becomes significant.

Entry into schools at an early age would not be a problem if the programs were developed to meet the needs of the children. To do this, the school needs to move to an approach to teaching and learning that recognizes the value of play as learning. It needs to recognize the tremendous contribution of play to the development of the whole child. It needs to provide staff for the early years that know and understand how children learn through play.

> *For further information on curriculum and other issues related to young children see the National Association for the Education of Young Children at* www.naeyc.org; *the Association for Childhood Education International at* www.acei.org; *and the Canadian Association for Young Children,* www.cayc.ca.

The trend over the past decade has been toward pushing a traditional teacher-directed program down into the kindergartens and even the preschools. Parents worry that their child won't be ready for school. They seek preschools that promise academic learning. They purchase books and kits that are sold under the guise of creating young geniuses. The pressure to hurry the introduction of school learning, along with the growing expectations for academic success, have given rise to concerns on the part of parents and teachers. An article in the *New York Times* in September 2007 reports on a practice called *red shirting*. This term, taken from sports, refers to the practice of parents holding children back a year so that they will be more mature and better able to deal with the demands of kindergarten. As the article points out, the gift of time this practice offers children, given the nature of today's kindergarten curriculum, has marked benefits for children.

The pushed-down expectations of the school system have had a profound effect on preschools. Where programs for the very young were once grounded in play and understanding of child development, today we see more and more of these facilities promoting academics over play.

I recently visited a preschool that was being advertised as having a program that emphasized computers as a way of giving young children a head start on academics. There were ten computers set up with several programs designed to teach reading readiness and mathematics to preschoolers. There was no home center, dress-up area, or large building blocks. Most of the toys were small and uninviting. I watched as the two- and three-year-olds sat at the computers. As I might have expected, they did not take any interest in the programs for readiness; rather they played with the computer, experimenting with making it go on and off and trying to get it to make noises. The children were quite isolated, with little opportunity to interact with others doing a similar activity. What a waste of a child's precious learning time. In another three to four years, these children would learn to use the computers in no time at all, with little effort, but the important lessons of play will have been squandered.

Over my long career, I have listened to many parents and teachers express concern about "wasting time" at play when there are so many things to learn. Parents fear that if children use their time during the preschool years playing, they will not be ready for kindergarten. Kindergarten teachers fear that if children don't do pencil and paper seatwork, they won't be ready for grade one. So pervasive is this notion that as the authors of an Ontario Ministry of Education report on early education (1983) commented, "It is as if we believe that over the magic summer between kindergarten and grade one, the child grows up and grows old." Although this was written a long time ago, unfortunately little has changed in this respect. If anything, there is more pressure to put aside play than ever before, not just in first grade but also in kindergarten and preschool.

Even educators who should know better do not seem to understand that it is not the child who ought to get ready for grade one, but that grade one ought to get ready for the child. I recently watched a segment on our local television news featuring a grade one class that was being provided with an "academic" program. When children in the class were interviewed, they remarked that, unlike kindergarten where you could play and have fun, now they had to "really work and do homework." When the principal was interviewed, she spoke proudly of the rigorous demands on the children in the name of preparing them for later success in school.

This thinking goes against a great deal of highly respected learning theory that suggests that development is central to establishing the foundation for learning. When everything is ready in a developmental sense, that is, the physical, emotional, and psychological dimensions are in place, children learn easily and well. When development is not as it ought to be, the result will be superficial learning that "masks a vacuum." And how does readiness in a developmental sense occur? It is the product of play. I often hear kindergarten teachers say, "We have no time for play. We have too much work to cover." What nonsense! Knowing what we do about play, it ought to be our priority, and if time is limited, the other stuff that we call work should be forfeited.

One evening I was doing a presentation to a parent group on the topic of play and learning. Throughout the talk I noticed two Japanese women directly in front of me. At the end of the talk, they headed toward me. They introduced themselves as mother and daughter. The elderly mother gave me a hug and said, "Oh, I wish my husband were here!" She then proceeded to tell me about a recent argument she and her husband had had with their daughter regarding the grandchildren. It seems that the grandfather, who was a retired university professor in Japan, often took care of the four-year-old grandson while the parents were at work. The child's mother was becoming increasingly anxious that her father spent too much time "just playing" with him. Several

15

days prior to my talk, she arrived home to find the grandfather and his grandson with tablecloths around their shoulders for capes, swooping about in Superman fashion. "You're a university professor," exclaimed the child's mother. "You should be teaching him something." As the mother and daughter were leaving, the daughter turned to me and said, "I feel as if I have a huge load taken off my shoulders. Thank you!"

Generally, as with this parent, it is with the best of intentions that parents push their children into inappropriate activities at the expense of play. They are bombarded by promises of academic excellence and of getting a jump on the competition. For the most part, what these programs offer is rote learning that has no roots. Like a plant that is rootless, it shoots up quickly and appears to be thriving, but without a root system to sustain this growth, in time it withers. The late Fredelle Maynard, a well-known Canadian journalist, attributed the stress parents feel to have their child get a jump on school to what she called "all the eggs in one basket." If you only have one child, Fredelle used to say, parents feel that he better be perfect.

Chart 1.1

SUMMARY OF CHALLENGES TO PLAY		
Erosion of childhood	**Society's attitudes toward play**	**Pushed-down curriculum**
• Turning children into mini adults • Excessive exposure to violence, sex, and negative family images • Commercial exploitation of children • Inappropriate clothing, toys, hair styles, and activities	• No learning value in play • Work ethic instilled early emphasizing rigor rather than fun • Emphasis on external motivation and accomplishments • Extrinsic rewards versus inner motivation and satisfaction – winning is everything	• Misunderstand nature of learning process • Emphasis on directed instruction • Pencil and paper tasks more valuable than play • Excess pressure to get ready for next level –learning becomes a race!

What Can We Do To Help?

> ➢ Simply being aware of the value of play and showing your child that you see play as important may not seem like much, but it will go a long way toward supporting learning through play.

> ➢ Resist the pressure to push your child ahead of herself. Let her have the advantage at each age and stage of enjoying childhood. It is not that young children cannot accomplish academic tasks at an early age. The point is: Why should they? What are they losing out on as they labor over memorizing number facts? What are the important basics for a three-year-old or a five-year-old?

> ➢ Support teachers and other parents who value play and don't want a watered-down grade one program for their four-year-old. If parents and teachers of young children worked together as advocates for children's right to play, we could stem the flood of practices that undermine learning through play.

Parents and teachers need to understand that play is learning and that establishing a foundation for academic success through play is far more important than rote learning of the ABCs or counting to ten. Once we have faith in the power of play, then we can delight in playing with our children and allowing them every opportunity to learn the consequential lessons of play. From Plato to contemporary scholars, the value of play has been explored.

"Is play the leading form of activity for a young child? It seems to me that from the point of view of development, play is not the predominant form of activity, but it is the leading source of development in pre-school years."

Lev Vygotsky

2

What Is Play?

Life is creative. It plays itself into existence, seeking out new relationships, new capacities, new traits. Life is an experiment to discover what's possible. As it tinkers with discovery, it creates more and more possibilities. With so much freedom for discovery, how can life be anything but playful?

Margaret Wheatley

What a wonderful description of play. As this quote suggests, play is a fundamental life force that gives rise to the creative impulse to explore new frontiers. Whether we are two days old, two years old, or nearing our last days, we continue to enjoy the mystery of play. We are never too old to be playful or to take advantage of the gifts that play offers to enrich our lives. When we talk about play in this way, we are describing a spontaneous, free, and joyous activity that is not controlled by the expectations and directives of others. Play is an activity freely undertaken for the value it brings in and of itself.

When is Play the Real Deal?

Although the content of play has changed over the years, the *process* remains largely untouched by time. Agreeing on a single definition of what play is has proven difficult. Each field of study has its own particular focus but generally when researchers speak of play they describe it as *active, absorbing, spontaneous, enjoyable, and undertaken without the pressure of either external approval or external rules.* These qualities are as evident today as they were in that long ago time of my childhood.

Given the attitude toward play in our society, it is not surprising that the term play is used often to mean activities that are anything but spontaneous and free. When we use the term "playing" a sport, for example, we generally think of a rule-bound, serious activity that is anything but playful. When playing hockey, children as young as six years old are expected to stick by the rules or risk expulsion. The frustration and anxiety shown by children under these circumstances shows how far this kind of activity is from the absorbing, intensely satisfying experiences of true play.

In order to understand the nature of real play, think back for a moment to your own childhood play. Where did you play? Whom did you play with? What did you play? Are there certain smells and feelings that come to you as you think back on your early play? I have found that when adults reminisce about play, there is a remarkable similarity about our recollections, even when we come from vastly different cultural backgrounds. I recently conducted some training sessions with an early childhood group. The twenty-six participants represented at least ten different cultural backgrounds, including China, Pakistan, and Brazil, as well as different parts of Canada. Settings were both rural and urban. When we compared our experiences, we were struck by how similar they were. We generally agreed that one of the best things about play was the freedom to do what we wanted. We relived the feeling of timelessness. We remembered that no one told us what we had to play. No one seemed to worry that we took on stereotypical characters from our favorite movie or TV program. In fact, adults seemed to have little or no interest in our play. We didn't play to please someone else. We played for the sake of playing.

No matter what form play takes, it is always *active*. When we watch our children playing, we see that play involves both physical and mental activity. With young children the physical aspect is most evident. When our children are at their most playful, they resemble whirling dervishes as they jump and run and sing. When physical activeness is curtailed, it will generally limit the play and often results in children ceasing to play at all. By middle childhood, much of the child's imaginative play may go on in the mind, unnoticed by those around her.

Perhaps the truest test of play is *absorption*. When children are truly into their play, nothing can distract them. How often have we heard a parent or teacher describe a young child as having a poor attention span? In play, there is no such thing. When a child is first introduced to new toys or new materials, she may sample several things before focusing on any one object. She may flit from item to item, trying them all out. Once she is caught up, however, in both mind and body, the absorption is astonishing. A child who does not exhibit absorption in play is generally a child with problems. Healthy children will lose themselves in their play and resent intrusion. When truly engaged, children won't be distracted. They are oblivious to everything else. Mom may be calling or the teacher announcing time to tidy up, but the children are too involved to respond.

Another quality that sets play apart from other similar activities is *spontaneity*. It is spontaneity that allows for the unexpected, the unplanned discovery. As we remember from our own play, this is a treasured quality that makes play memorable. We played when we wanted to and what we wanted to. No one came along and said, "All right, you can play now!" If they did, we likely would not have bothered. It is this characteristic that makes the popular term *directed play* such an anomaly. This term is used to suggest that while we say that we value play, we don't trust it to be worthwhile unless we control it. Once we begin to control it by dictating what children can play, with whom, and for how long, play is no longer play.

Play is usually thought of first and foremost as an *enjoyable* activity. When I first began to study children's play, I was often puzzled by their seriousness toward what went on. While play is enjoyable, there are moments of tension and anger as children negotiate complex, dramatic play, but this does not take away from the satisfaction children experience when conflicts are resolved and the play soars. It is my feeling that *satisfaction* is a truer indicator of play than enjoyment. Perhaps they are one and the same, but it seems helpful to make this distinction when deciding whether or not the activity is truly play.

Play is undertaken *without regard for external approval or rules*. Children play because they want to. No one has to tell them when to play or how to play. It is as natural as breathing to them. Play offers its own rewards, the most powerful of which is satisfaction. When we offer external rewards for how or what children play, it no longer is the natural activity that enriches the whole child. From infancy, a baby plays without being told by us what to do. It is instinctive for a baby to touch and taste and handle everything that comes her way. Highly active play brings satisfaction and delight, as it will throughout childhood. Play satisfies personal needs within the child that an adult may not understand but that are essential to growth and development.

Features That Make a Difference

Several other important features mark the play of young children. Play is instinctive, interactive, repetitive, and inventive. These features are found in all forms of play and across developmental and cultural boundaries.

Play is instinctive. No one shows a baby how to put her foot in her mouth or the toddler how to make mud pies. The brain is programmed to learn and from the outset learning is *self-directed*, that is, the incentive to explore comes from within the infant and not as a result of someone directing the infant to perform. What, then, is the role of the parent or caregiver? We support learning through exploration by providing appropriate toys and experiences. We play with the baby, showing her how a toy, such as a rattle, works. We validate with smiles and hugs when the baby shows some new learning, and we keep her safe. A baby naturally reaches out to learn through play, but subsequent experiences can either encourage or discourage instinctive exploration. This is particularly evident in the toddler years when the child has the mobility to go farther afield. It takes patience on the part of parents to encourage instinctive play.

Play is interactive. From the first day of birth, learning through play soars in the presence of a loving parent or caregiver. Interaction with siblings and other extended family members as well as friends is important to early play and learning. Grandparents, for example, often have games and songs that bring tradition to the learning. Grandparents may have more time than busy parents to spend playing with the baby. Babies tend to take an early interest in older brothers and sisters, wanting to be able to do what they do. This provides a powerful incentive for the baby to crawl and to talk.

Through interaction, young children develop the social skills that are a prerequisite to being a good play partner. In turn, play enables children to learn the life skills that are necessary for healthy participation in a social environment. Through interaction in play, a baby begins to learn such things as making and maintaining eye contact as well as turn taking. Anyone who has played with a baby knows that this is not instinctive. Babies are very impatient.

Grandpa begins to untie the boat in preparation for going out. Paxton watches and quickly begins to bounce up and down, making impatient squawks. As Grandpa takes his time preparing the boat, Paxton becomes increasingly frustrated and his actions more frenetic.

Interaction through play leads to dramatic development in communication and subsequently language skills. Communicating pleasure, anger, and other feelings is learned as a young child plays.

As much as exploration and learning are instinctive, babies who are deprived of social contact soon become passive and unresponsive to their environment. Several years ago, a friend of mine adopted a baby from Siberia. The baby girl had not been abused nor in a sense abandoned, but her birth parents simply could not provide the basic needs of food and shelter for her. Her environment in the facility was quite sterile with few toys and few opportunities to interact with adults. At nine months she showed little interest in things around her and was quite timid in responding. Developmentally, she was not as far along as others of a similar age in either movement or language. Fortunately for her, she was adopted into a wonderful family where she was surrounded with love and a rich environment for play and learning.

Play is repetitive. Repetition is an important part of learning through play at all stages. A child will stack blocks up, knock them over, and start again. The two-year-old will take all the pots and pans out of the cupboard. Mom puts them back, and the toddler takes them out again! To the adult this seems like a waste of energy, but to the child, it is a way of confirming the predictability of actions. Trial and error is the child's way of learning how to make things happen. Once she discovers what an object can do, she will repeat this action over and over to see how it can be applied to other objects. The baby learns over time and with experience that shaking a rattle makes a noise, but the stuffed toy does not. She learns that a ball will roll when pushed, but a block won't. These understandings may seem insignificant to adults, but to the young child they are serious business.

Play is inventive. In play, children invent new worlds, new people, and new experiences using bits and pieces of the real world as they know it. While children try on roles from everyday life, they experiment with these roles to see what they can do and be. When we think of play, we think of make-believe, freedom, and humor. We do not so much associate the word *play* with scientific discovery, problem solving, or other similar inventions. Yet play is of the essence of all of these most valued skills.

Play engages the mind in ways that nothing else can. As humans we know that the creative power of imagination is what separates us from all other living beings. Play sets the imagination in motion and provides the opportunity for creative power to grow and strengthen with time and experience. Imagination gives birth to the arts, to scientific discovery, and to social reform. It is the catalyst for all great human endeavors. Without imagination there would be no space exploration, nor solutions found for the profound dilemmas facing our planet today. The demands upon our collective imagination as humans sharing global resources are staggering. This kind of imagination cannot be taught by traditional academic means but can be nurtured through play. Play in this sense is not trivial but of utmost importance in the long-term education of our children. A constant dimension of play is that it is free and full of possibility.

How Well Does Your Child Play?

We assume that because play is such a natural activity of childhood that all children play well. Given the characteristics just described, it is clear that what we refer to as play is often anything but. When children are enrolled in too many structured activities, even though they may be called play, they do not develop the capacity to direct their own play and therefore lack spontaneity, absorption, and satisfaction. These are the children who are bored when faced with time to play on their own. They do not seem to know how to go about this. Is it any wonder if at every turn they have been directed, that given the freedom to play, they will turn to watching TV or using a computer game that requires little more than pushing buttons? It is not a sign of maturity when a child prefers to do worksheets and school-like activities rather than play. It means that she does not know how to play.

The benefits of play to development and learning depend on how well your child plays. You may need to invest more time playing with her. You can make use of community programs that are already established.

Chart 2.1

HOW WELL DOES MY CHILD PLAY?
A Summary of the Characteristics

If you want to know how well your child plays stand back and watch while she is playing with other children. Ask the following questions:

More Able Players	Less Able Players
• Is she physically active? • Is she absorbed in her play? • Does she stay with the activity? • Does she tune out everything else? • Does she play with others, sharing space, toys, and cooperating? • Does she use talk to control others? To resolve conflict? To speak in the voice of her pretend character? • Does she show a sense of humor in her play through her actions? Through her talk?	• Does she sit back and watch others? • Is she easily distracted and flits from one thing to another? • Does she play alone and resist getting involved with others? • Does she resort to physical means of getting her way during play? • Is she serious and non-playful most of the time?

A brief mention must be made here about children with disabilities. It has been my experience that often the children who most need play are deprived of this opportunity and therefore don't learn to play. The assumption is made that either they are unable to play, especially with others, or that they need to be doing directed pencil-and-paper activities that are assumed to provide an academic foundation.

One morning I was observing Melinda, a child with Down Syndrome. I watched her play alone with a doll. As I walked over, she said, "Dolly sick." She rocked her dolly back and forth and then handed her to me. "Doctor," she said as she picked up a play doctor's bag and began to examine her dolly. We had quite an extensive conversation in role, she as the doctor, and me as the mom.

I don't know how long this might have lasted because the classroom teacher interrupted and took Melinda off to a table where she was to color a picture, a task she found frustrating and of little interest. I spoke with the teacher and tried to explain what she was learning through our play experience, but obviously the traditional notion of teacher-

directed activity taking precedence over play was well entrenched in this teacher's practice.

It was quite some time before I once again got back to that room. As soon as I walked through the door, Melinda jumped up from her chair and ran over. "Play! Play" she said. "Okay," I replied. "Where are the dolls?" I asked as I looked around. Most of the toys had been removed, including the dolls, but as I watched, Melinda went to a cupboard and, struggling, pulled out a box in the bottom of which were her precious dolls. With glares from the teacher, Melinda and I had a wonderful session of play. She used language well in conversation; she took on her role as mom with authenticity and even invited another little girl to join us. Sadly, the teacher was not convinced, and Melinda did not thrive in school as she might have.

Studies (Odam, McConnell, and Chandler 1993) have shown that some children who have disabilities may in fact be quite similar in their play behavior to those without disabilities, especially with respect to language. Children with autistic disorders may, however, lack the spontaneity, symbolic thinking, and language to participate in sociodramatic play (Jarrod, Boucher, and Smith 1996). While this may be true, I recall that one master's of education student with whom I worked conducted a study of older autistic children and found that these older children flourished when allowed to play. Given the opportunity to play in the water, where their movements became less rigid, there was a remarkable difference in the children's body language and behavior. These children smiled and laughed. Play with special needs children is an area that requires more comprehensive research. What we can be sure of is that no child, disabled or otherwise, can be harmed by play.

What Can We Do To Help?

> ➢ Remember that to play means to be fully absorbed, to be
>   actively involved, to imagine, to interact with others, and to
>   be free.

➢ Sports and computer games can be an extension of play, but the benefits to development and learning come from play that is spontaneous and driven by the child's inner needs.

➢ All children need play. Those with disabilities should not be deprived of this invaluable learning experience. Children have a wonderful way of compensating for their disabilities, and this may be the only way some children can learn how to get along in the world.

Play is as old as time itself. All creatures, animal and human, play so as to learn the lessons of life. Few activities have more value across the life span of an individual, and the lessons of play from childhood remain a lifetime.

3
How Children Play

Of all the formulations of play, perhaps the briefest and the best is found in Plato's Laws. Plato sees the model of true playfulness in the need of all young, animal and human, to leap.

Erik Erikson

Young children learn through three kinds of play—exploratory play, pretend play, and games with rules. Beginning around age four, a unique type of pretend play emerges that we refer to as *sociodramatic play*. As the label implies, it involves both social and dramatic aspects. This type of pretend play continues until somewhere around age eight and gradually gives way to improvisation and what is more traditionally understood as drama.

Each type of play starts at birth and can be seen at each stage of development, with important changes occurring to coincide with major developmental milestones. Starting to crawl and walk, for example, serves as a major impetus for exploratory play. With mobility comes the opportunity to go beyond the immediate world, thus opening up vast possibilities for exploration. The development of talk and communication provides further means of extending the boundaries of play by allowing the child to enter the social world of others.

Children show preferences for the kind of play, as well as the materials they choose. Some children are more drawn to exploring and building than to the dress-up of pretend play. Others prefer pretend play. The richest play generally comes when children combine these forms of play, that is, they build a bus and then pretend to go on a journey. It is typical to see children go through a period of exploration before using an unfamiliar object for pretend play. They may move back and forth depending upon their inner needs of the moment.

Chart 3.1

HOW CHILDREN PLAY: A SUMMARY	
There are a number of ways of talking about the forms of play but play activities generally fall into three types of activity - exploration, pretend play and games.	
Forms	**Characteristics**
Exploratory Play	• Begins in infancy and continues through childhood • Involves all five senses: taste, touch, smell, sight, and hearing • Includes physical activities such as jumping, climbing, and running
Pretend Play Socio-dramatic Play	• Begins at age 2 and continues • Starts as child make-believes he is someone or something develops into reenacting familiar activities such as feeding the baby • Begins between age 4 - 5 • Involves more than one player • Based upon everyday experiences
Games With Rules	• Most preschoolers ignore rules or make them up as they go along • Age seven begins the obsession with "playing fair", by which children mean playing by the rules.

Exploratory Play

A baby begins the journey of learning through *exploratory play*. It is as if the baby is asking, "What is it?" While some play experts make a distinction between play and exploration, this early process of discovery is in a real sense play. Exploratory play is a spontaneous, active, enjoyable experience that carries its own rewards for the baby. Through exploratory play, a young child makes use of his five senses (sight, taste, touch, sound, and smell) to investigate the world he has entered. The exploratory play of young children is highly physical, using all of the child's body to learn.

Sound is the first sense to be awakened. There is evidence that before birth, the fetus responds to sounds, in particular the sound of the mother's voice, as well as music and familiar everyday noises from the environment. Even before birth, babies are able to distinguish familiar voices. Once born, babies use this remarkable sense to imitate the sounds of language and make noises that lead to important learning about the nature of objects. A rattle sounds different from the banging of a spoon. The rattle only makes a noise when it is shaken. By surrounding the baby with music and talk, we promote the development of this sensory ability.

Healthy babies do not wait passively for us to "teach" them how to learn through exploration. From the moment they are born, babies are busy every waking moment as they taste and touch everything within reach. Infants explore their own bodies, putting their fingers, toes, and anything else they can find in their mouths. They intently watch objects such as the mobile over the crib or the movement of a pet. Babies explore objects within reach by touching, tasting, and watching whatever is there. Over the first few months of life, babies discover an amazing amount of information through exploratory play. They learn to identify people and things. They begin to learn what they can do with common, everyday objects as well as toys.

Once a baby begins to crawl, there are huge spurts of learning through *exploratory play*. He is now intent not only in finding out "what it is?" but "what can I do with it?" Toddlers find all kinds of novel ways to use everyday objects. As children explore, they learn about space and such notions as up and down and under and over. They learn that even though an object is out of sight, it still exists. This is the foundation upon which mathematics and science will be developed. They learn about the people and things around them and where they themselves fit in. These lessons provide the basis for understanding who they are and how to take their place in a social world. These understandings about the world cannot be taught by any other means than through self-directed play.

Chart 3.2

EXPLORATORY PLAY AND SENSORY STIMULATION				
Newborns are already equipped with the ability to learn through sensory stimulation. They react to noise and smell and taste. They respond to touch. They follow the movement of an object. Providing a rich supply of materials and experiences that stimulate exploratory play will greatly enhance sensory development.				
Visual	Auditory	Tactile	Taste	Smell
Indoor: • Lights with colored shades& bulbs • Mirror • Mobiles • Pictures and wall hangings • Sun catcher	Toys: • Rattle, squeak toys Music: • Singing, CDs, DVDs Instruments: • Drum • tambourine, harmonica	Natural materials: • Wood, sand, water, leaves, feathers, fur Cloth: • Velvet, corduroy, silk, leather	Foods that taste sweet: • Sugar, honey, maple syrup, fruit Sour: • Lemon, vinegar, pickles	Indoor: • Cooking foods, pot pourie, herbs, spices • laundry, cleaning products
Outdoor: • Flowers, trees, animals, signs, vehicles, insects, and bugs	Outdoors • Rain, traffic, animal sounds Indoor: • Vacuum, mixer, grinder	Man-made materials: • Aluminum foil, rubber, waxed paper, soap	Foods that taste bitter: • Rappini, • Bitter chocolate Salty: • Salted nuts, cured meats	Outdoor: • Leaves, grass, flowers, garbage, pine needles

By age four, exploratory play is soaring. Children who have been encouraged to explore freely and without undue restriction will continue to learn through exploring an increasingly broad range of unfamiliar objects and materials. Sand, water, and other natural materials continue to hold endless fascination.

I visited a senior kindergarten classroom one morning. Five-year-old Ethan, who was usually to be found at the home center, was playing at the water table. When he saw me, he called over, "Come and see this. It's amazing!" Over I went to find Ethan pouring water from a small beaker into a larger pail. "Look," he said, "it always takes eight of these to fill the big one."

Afterward the teacher shared her concern that Ethan had been playing at the water table every day that week, doing what she perceived as a "baby" activity. "Should I have moved him to another area?" she asked. I asked her why she had let him stay there every day. "Well," she replied, "he was so interested in what he was doing that I figured he must be learning something important to him."

Although not sure what, she recognized the value in letting Ethan direct his own learning. On reflection, she saw that he was discovering some very sophisticated understandings about the nature of liquids and realized his need to confirm his findings over and over again in order to firmly establish this concept in his mind.

Exploratory play is the basis for scientific inquiry. It is born of the impulse to create new and better ways of doing things. During the middle years, children continue to learn through exploration as they move out into an increasingly complex world. Anyone who has a child ages nine to twelve knows that there is nothing they enjoy more than taking things apart and trying to put them back together. This is the hold that interlocking blocks have on children right into their teen years. Similarly at the beach, it is not only the very young who dig in the sand but children of all ages. Usually the dad is more engrossed in building the sandcastle than the three-year-old, who would rather run in the sand and throw it in the air than build something.

Preschoolers are experts at exploration, and adults should make sure that they nurture this wonderful ability by providing an emotional environment that encourages initiative, curiosity, and problem solving. Placing too much emphasis on the end product, on using tools and materials the correct way, and on discouraging noise or mess undermines exploration and creates an atmosphere in which the child loses confidence in his ability. If we want to avoid "cookie-cutter" people, we need to place high value on exploratory play and celebrate the children's discoveries at every opportunity.

Pretend Play

The second form of play is *pretend play*. We introduce pretend play to our baby when we play games such as This Little Piggy Went to Market. The toes are not "piggies," but in the game, it is as if they were. "Rock-A-Bye Baby" and other similar rhymes create similar situations for make-believe with the baby. It will be around fifteen months, however, before we see a child initiate pretend play.

Self-directed, spontaneous pretend play begins when a toddler uses one object to represent another. An object such as a piece of wood is used *as if* it were a car or a hammer or any number of other familiar objects. The child knows the difference between the objects but pretends otherwise. When a child plays like this, he shows that he can represent an object with something else. This signals a milestone of development in the brain. This is called *representational thinking* and is the basis for language, for problem solving, and all higher forms of human mental activity.

In the earliest pretend play, children imitate actions they see in everyday life. Fifteen-month-old Tatum places her baby doll in the stroller. She hangs her purse over the handle and takes off for a walk with her baby.

Young children rely on what they know and understand of the world as a resource for their pretend play. They do, however, use imagination to rework everyday events into their own personal world of pretending. In the midst of the pretend walk, Tatum throws the dolly out and piles blocks into the stroller.

During the toddler years, play becomes increasingly social. Toddlers often play side by side, sharing space, toys, and equipment. At this stage they love pretend play, but each child develops his own series of actions.

Three-year-old Liam and Hugo are playing Superman. Both swoop and dart around the room independent of one another. They do some interacting, but each stays with the superhero role. It does not matter that they are both the same character performing almost the same actions. Each is caught up in his own make-believe world.

Similarly, if we watch children at this age playing house, each child plays out his own story, even though several are playing together.

Toddlers are often scolded for not sharing during their play when in fact this is an unrealistic expectation. At this stage, each child is focused on his own play and becomes quite frustrated if another child disrupts him. In the absence of adequate language, children will tend to either resolve the conflict using physical aggression or turn to an adult to solve their problem. It is these skirmishes, however, that provide the basis for learning how to cooperate, and we are generally better off to let our children resolve the conflict themselves than to disrupt them and take away a valuable learning experience.

By age three, children are well into make-believe but still lack the social skills and perhaps the language to make this a collaborative endeavor. Children want adults as play partners although not as true participants.

While visiting friends one evening, three-year-old Sonia invited me to join her in her playhouse. She directed me to sit down at the child-size table.

"Let's call up Wonder Woman," she said, "and invite her over for coffee."

Sonia then picked up the toy telephone and pretended to make a phone call.

"Hello," she said. "Is this Wonder Woman? Susie and I want you to come for coffee. See ya! Bye."

Sonia then draped a large scarf over her shoulders and pretended to be Wonder Woman. As she talked back and forth to herself in one role and then the other, I asked her, "But who am I?"

"You're Susie," Sonia exclaimed in surprise, as if to say, who else would I be!

Throughout the half hour of play I was never engaged in a role, but when I attempted to leave, Sonia's disappointment was evident.

Sometime between ages four and five, a very important change occurs when a child begins to collaborate with others in creating episodes of pretend play. While several players may take on the same role, there is a distinct development of the story with each character contributing. This form of play is called *sociodramatic play.*

> *An episode of sociodramatic play is a sequence of make-believe in which two or more players collaborate to construct roles and actions around a common theme. The episode begins when the players signal a transformation, either through an explicit statement or an implicit action. An episode continues so long as two players remain with the theme. It ends when all the players abandon the theme or time runs out.*

The fluid nature of sociodramatic play makes it hard for onlookers to understand what is going on. It is play but it is not *a* play. It does not have a clear beginning, middle, or end as a play has. Nor does it have a cast of characters with clearly identifiable roles. In playing house, for example, you find three mothers and no fathers or one father and two mothers. The players remain true to the actual activities: the table is set, and food is prepared and served. Dora feeds her dolly with a spoon, baths her in the sink, wraps her in a towel, and burps her. So authentic are these actions that it seems as though there really is water in the sink and actual baby food on the spoon.

At this stage children generally move back and forth between male and female roles. The boys are as likely to put on the high-heeled shoes or the fancy dress as the girls are. Even having a baby is not reserved for females as I noticed one morning while playing in a senior kindergarten room.

Paolo has been brought into the hospital following a pretend accident. As he lies there, Sonia stuffs a dolly under his sweater and tells him, "It's your turn to have the baby today!" Shortly thereafter, Luke yanks the dolly out and hands it to Paolo with great fanfare. He proceeds to rock the dolly in his arms and gently kisses it on the top of the head.

Sociodramatic play is so familiar that parents rarely pay any attention to it. Yet it is an amazingly complex activity, placing higher demands on social development and language than almost any other activity. If we would stop and unobtrusively watch and listen, we would learn a great deal about our children. We would see how our children think and feel and what issues are troubling them.

Games With Rules

The third form of play is *games with rules*. Games that we play with young children have the general features of all play, that is, they are spontaneous, enjoyable, and satisfy inner needs but with the addition of rules. Piaget saw games with rules as an advanced form of childhood play in which young children were unable to participate. I suggest, however, that the informal *action games* that we play with babies are the earliest form of games with rules. Games such as peekaboo and This Little Piggy Went to Market have rules in that they are played the same way all the time. There may be minor variations, but there is a set pattern of action, and this pattern is in a real sense the "rule."

The action games that we play with babies are passed down from one generation to another. The physical actions of early games are predictable and repetitive. Clapping, tickling, bouncing, rocking, and swinging are typical actions that make up these first games. Usually a rhyme or a song accompanies the repetitive actions of games. These rhymes may be taken from folklore or be spontaneously made up as adults play with babies.

In North American culture, many action games have their origins in the Mother Goose rhymes. Such old standards as "Rock-a-Bye Baby" quickly become familiar to the baby, and the giggles and smiles that light up the baby's face give proof of the value of such games.

Studies have shown that the same patterns of action exist across all cultures. Many cultures have single action games, such as tickling the infant, as well as repetitive games using clapping, rocking, and swinging actions. These games are played using a pattern that teaches the child about predictability. From early on, action games such as pat-a-cake may involve coordination. Others help a very young child learn about her body.

A Trinidadian mom was playing with her baby. She placed ten-month-old Anoushka in front, facing her. She held the baby's hands in hers and tapped Anoushka's index fingers together several times as she chanted, "Little bird fly, fly, fly, fly." She then moved one index finger to touch Anoushka's nose, chanting, "Fly to the top of Anoushka's nose." She ended the game by tickling Anoushka's belly button and giving her a hug. She told me that she would repeat this game many times throughout a day, ending on different parts of Anoushka's body.

Variations of this game exist in many cultures, but while all parents play similar games, there are differences that reflect their cultural experiences. Games have been described as "culturally developed parenting programs." Such universal games as peekaboo or pat-a-cake and the West Indian classic Brown Girl in the Ring provide important opportunities for the parent to interact with the baby by touching, showing affection, and making sustained eye contact. These important play interactions help the infant to become a loving, cooperative human being.

Toddlers want to have play partners. Simple games of tag and hide-and-seek are among the first action games involving other players. The rules are quite simple and are changed by the children on a whim.

Ball games are closely tied to physical development and coordination and before age four can be very frustrating for a child. It is helpful to remember that a three-year-old can throw a ball well before he can catch one. The coordination needed to hit a ball with a bat or a hockey stick is beyond most preschoolers.

By school age, children enjoy action games involving winning and losing. Such favorites as Sally Go Round the Sun and London Bridge introduce children to following prescribed rules. Action games such as Red Rover introduce teams with the added demands for cooperation that this requires. These kinds of action games continue into the middle years and help prepare children for team sports, where rules are strictly enforced and winning becomes the goal. Competition in the early action games is not as we generally think of it, that is, with winners and losers, although there does seem to be a quality of "winning" even in the games of babies. Winning in this sense means achieving a goal. In peekaboo, for example, the goal is to see the object reappear. Later on this kind of goal achievement is seen in games such London Bridge or Ring Around the Rosie.

Action games are a valuable source of learning across all areas of development from infancy throughout childhood. Games that adults play with infants are a source of bonding and the beginnings of positive social interaction. As games become more elaborate and play partners become involved, games offer a nonthreatening way of learning the valuable social skills of turn taking, cooperation, and communication. It goes without saying that action games are a rich resource for physical development, in particular gross motor development. Action games help children to understand space and such notions as in and out, over and under, and so on.

Between ages four and five, children begin to take an interest in board games. There are basically two types of board games: those that involve matching and those that use a pathway. One of the simplest board games using matching is a *form board* that consists of a board with the outline of several objects on it and a set of matching manipulatives, one for each outline. There are commercial form boards made out of wood that have cutaways of several objects on the board with a set of matching objects. The easiest form boards have quite large distinct objects that a young child can readily discriminate, such as animals. Form boards with a series of graduated objects large to small are readily available as are form boards using geometric shapes. A more challenging type of matching board is one that requires the player to match pictures that vary only in less obvious ways. These kinds of matching tasks are believed to help children learn visual discrimination as well as the classification and sorting abilities fundamental to reading and math.

Board games using a *pathway* can be as simple as Candyland or as complex as Monopoly. The easiest pathway games are ones in which each player has a board with a simple path on it, counters to mark each step as they move along the path, and a spinner or die with no more than three dots. To increase the challenge, children can share one board and take turns with the die. By age five, the children may be ready for a ten-sided die or may be using a pair of dice where two sets of numbers are added. The challenges increase as more rules are added, as for example, in Snakes and Ladders. These more difficult games require cooperation and turn taking and therefore are more suited to older primary children.

Board games have specific rules that determine how the game is played, but these rules do not inhibit the way the three-year-old plays. Three-year-olds make their own rules, changing them as they go in order to win. This is not cheating as adults might assume but rather an entirely age-appropriate way of playing. It is around age seven that children become very aware of the rules and, as any parent or second grade teacher knows, the phrase "it's not fair" becomes all too familiar.

A three-year-old friend of mine, Bella, had a board game from a local fast-food restaurant. It involved a two-track path and a cube numbered one to four. As we neared the finish line, I needed three and rolled four. I declared myself the winner. "No, you're not," she said. "You've got to go around again." She then rolled the die and announced, "I won." We played quite a few games and every single time, she won! I've observed this many times and remind parents and teachers that this is not a sign of cheating but simply the nature of competition in three-year-olds.

40

Preschoolers may play a board game alongside one another without regard for competition. Unlike games as adults understand them, competition does not need to be part of the games of the very young. These games are generally played simply for the fun of it. The enjoyment is the reward, not the winning. By age seven children become quite competitive.

Card games have always had a special place in childhood play. From the simple matching card game of lotto that three-year-olds play to games such as Fish or Old Maid, card games are part of the family traditions in many homes. With the proliferation of computer games, family-oriented games are at risk of disappearing. Setting aside time for the whole family to play either a board or a card game is one positive way of preserving the social life of a family. As with board games, how children respond to the rules depends upon their development and experience. Playing card games that require sticking to rules is best left until school age.

Chart 3.3

GAMES THAT DEVELOP THE MIND		
Game Genres	**Samples**	**Skills**
Action Games	• This Little Piggy • This Old Man • London Bridge	• Counting • Following a sequence • Spatial understanding • Patterning
Board Games	• Matching Games (e.g., form boards, jigsaw puzzles) • Pathways (e.g., using 1 die, using two dice)	• Matching shapes • Spatial relations • Problem solving • Counting • One-to-one correspondence • Following directions
Card Games	• Lotto • Fish	• Distinguishing similarities and differences • Sorting by properties of shape, color or size

Games are important not only to the development of the mind but also to the emotional and affective well-being of the young child. When parents play games with their children, they behave differently than in other situations. For example, it has been observed that when directly trying to teach a young child something related to school, such as his colors or the ABCs, the parent is likely to become punitive and scolding when the child does not get it. On the other hand, when playing games, the parent and child giggle and hug and take mistakes in stride.

What Can We Do to Help?

➤ Children learn how to play by playing. Encourage them to explore their environment, play with a variety of toys and materials, and enjoy pretending. Make sure that your child has the toys and materials to enjoy all forms of play. While all forms of play can stimulate physical, intellectual, and social development, each has particular lessons to be learned.

➤ Don't be afraid of the mess and noise created when play is in high gear. One young family I know has turned their living room into a "playroom." When visitors come, the toys are pushed aside and there is plenty of room for family and friends. As the mom said, "It will return to being a place to entertain once the girls are bigger, but right now they come first!"

➤ Games with rules need not be competitive. In fact, for young children the aspect of competition is more likely to be a goal such as completing a game of lotto rather than seeing who can get the most pairs.

Children play with vigor and enthusiasm. They never get tired of play that is of their own making. Each form of has its own sets of rules known instinctively to children. Each form of play changes as children grow and develop. While in time children are likely to find one or another form most satisfying, healthy children tend to use all three forms to meet their developmental needs.

Infants are world-class learners and can be
trusted to select, more or less on their own,
experiences that will enhance their learning.

Elizabeth Spelke
in an interview with Margaret Talbot

4
Learning through Play: The Body and the Mind

There seems to be a common assumption, in thinking about children's development, that earlier is better. So, the reasoning goes, if it's good for a four-year-old to understand counting, it would be even better if a two-year-old could be induced to understand counting. There is no evidence to support this assumption and some reason to be skeptical of it.

Elizabeth Spelke
in an interview with Margaret Talbot

Play has been described as the primary way children learn that which no one could teach them. By this it is meant that through the various forms of play, children learn the most critical lessons of life without directly being taught. These lessons are the foundation for all later learning, including mathematics and literacy.

The direct link between development, learning, and play has been well documented. The major advantage of learning through play is the natural way in which play addresses all areas of development in an integrated way without sacrificing any of the child's needs.

Play Develops the Body

The benefits to the body from the physical aspects of play come about through movement that is inherent in play. By definition, play is active. It provides the means for working every part of the body in an integrated way. Play is the best physical fitness program there is.

There are many health-related benefits of play:

- As children climb and swing and perform other weight-bearing movements, optimal bone development occurs.

- As children exert energy running, jumping, and dancing, there is an increase in oxygen to the muscles, which translates into cardiovascular health.

- Studies on brain function tell us that the brain is much more active during physical activity than when sitting passively. The physical experience of play stimulates the brain, causing learning to occur in every aspect of development.

In addition to health benefits, physical play contributes to social and emotional well-being.

- Physical achievement leads to competence and confidence. Just watch the beaming pride as your toddler takes his first independent steps!

- Physical movement through play also contributes to having a positive body image. Children who move with grace and coordination are much more likely to feel good about their self-image than those who do not.

- Physical competence leads to feelings of control and effectiveness.

- Physical play has obvious benefits for social development. We see children in the playground cluster around the most physically adept child. She will be the first pick for the team in the middle years and the sports hero of high school. Studies show that even in preschool, children with physical ability are the most popular with their peers.

As physical development proceeds, a young child learns to move her body with ease and handle such things as a juice cup in a controlled way. These achievements require the coordination of two muscle groups. Gross motor skills refer to the large muscles that control the torso, arms, and legs. These are the first muscles the baby develops as she tries to lift her head and control her neck muscles. She will control her arms before her fingers and the legs before her feet. One of the earliest actions of the fine muscles is the pincer grip that a baby uses to grasp the toys on her play station or to grab her mommy's hair. During the early days and months of life, learning is very physical.

Gross motor skills *involve large muscle activities, such as moving the arms and walking.*

Fine motor skills *involve movements using fine muscles, such as moving the fingers to handle cutlery.*

Both gross motor and fine motor skills develop as a result of a wide variety of play activities. A baby stretches, bounces, waves arms, and reaches out in the course of playing. As she plays pat-a-cake, she develops coordination. Every playful movement is directed toward learning and development. As children become mobile, play becomes increasingly physical, and the learning that goes on encompasses social and emotional well-being as well as physical competence.

By eight months children are quite mobile. They are able to climb stairs and have discovered their feet. They need to bounce up and down and push with their feet. As soon as children find their feet, they are on the move. This movement is part and parcel of play. The spontaneous jumping, running, and climbing that are so much part of how children move give rise to these many benefits. It does not matter whether indoors or out, whether at home or in the mall, children find things to hop up on and, later on, jump off. They find things to climb and things to swing upon. As a toddler grows, her movements become increasingly coordinated and adventuresome. The confidence to try new things comes with successful mastery of basic everyday tasks such as walking and feeding herself. Child development experts believe that motor activity during the second year of life, when children are beginning to walk, is vital to development and that few restrictions should be placed on their movement except, of course, for safety.

The physical aspects of play are spurred on by the introduction of toys and equipment that require increased coordination. Playground equipment and ride-on toys are among the most valuable toys for gross motor development. Paint brushes and scissors, interlocking blocks, play dough, and form puzzles are among the toys that help develop fine motor skills.

Competence in physical ability comes about through repeated experience and proceeds at an individual pace and in predictable stages. A toddler walks before she runs, throws a ball before she can catch one, and hits a ball off a tee before she can hit a pitched ball. Foundational skills must be developed before these skills can be directed toward an organized goal.

The process of learning physical skills through play is like any other significant human achievement. It does not follow a set of prescribed lessons but is a steady progress toward automatic performance, with many mishaps on the way. In her book, *Your Active Child*, Rae Pica (2003) cites the American Academy of Pediatrics to describe how competence is to be developed:

> *During the preschool years, motor skills are best learned in an unstructured, non-competitive setting in which a child can experiment and learn by trial and error on an individual basis. Specific skills can be refined through repetitive practice only after the relevant level of motor development has been reached.*

Play is not a race nor is it a competition. In play, the child is only competing with himself. Nowhere is this more evident than in physical development.

Play Develops the Mind

How the brain develops has been the source of study for decades. While we know a great deal about the workings of the brain, much of the brain activity remains a mystery. We do know, however, that between birth and age six, the brain grows more rapidly than at any other time in its development. In fact, it is believed that the brain reaches 50 percent of its capacity by age four, 30 percent by age eight, and 20 percent between the ages of eight and seventeen.

> "The brain gobbles up the external environment through the sensory system and then reassembles the digested world in the form of trillions of connections which are constantly growing or dying, becoming stronger or weaker depending upon the richness of the banquet."
>
> Richard Kotulak

While there is a fixed pattern to the way the brain develops, learning is the result of experiences that take place within a stimulating environment. To many this means play. In other words, what the child learns is the result of the play opportunities provided, the materials available, as well as the attitudes and actions of parents toward play.

A baby's brain is stimulated through sensory exploration. As a baby has repeated experiences, connections begin to form that are the basis for learning. What these experiences do is make pathways between the neurons, or nerve cells. The brain is constantly forming pathways of learning and with each new experience, not only are new connections made, but also existing pathways are re-formed to accommodate new learning. The role of play in this process is thought to be critical.

From birth, children are able to explore and come to understand cause and effect. This is a major underpinning of thinking and reasoning. Spurred on by curiosity, infants and toddlers use exploratory play to check out the world. As she does so, a baby begins to make connections between what she sees, hears, tastes, smells, and touches. Watch your baby play with a rattle. She learns that by shaking it, noises are made. She learns from putting it in her mouth that it doesn't taste good, like cookies, or gritty like dirt. She discovers the properties of the rattle through touching, tasting, moving, and watching it and the difference between this object and the many others in her world. Similar actions are repeated over and over as the baby plays with a wide variety of objects. Out of the learning that takes place comes understanding. As adults, we are far removed from the wonder of discovery in everyday life, but to the very young each new day brings wonderful discoveries.

Pleasure is a strong motivator for learning. A happy experience will provide the motivation to go the next step. When learning takes place through play, it provides pleasure and satisfaction. There's no need for tangible rewards such as stickers or candies. Children are not afraid of failure or of disappointing a parent. Vigorous mental activity depends on a positive emotional climate and general well-being. Play provides a climate that offers a safe place to take risks and learn the consequences of behavior.

In the early stages of life, exploratory play stimulates brain development. As a toddler matures, pretend play and sociodramatic play become a rich resource for the development of the mind. Games with rules offer enjoyable opportunities to expand and use mathematical understanding.

Through exploratory play, infants and toddlers begin to classify things in the immediate environment. They come to understand how objects are similar as well as different. In the early stage, the differences will be general, so that all animals, for example, are called dogs. By age six, children who have been around dogs can tell the difference between a Labrador retriever and a terrier. At the same time, they will be refining the language needed to describe and identify these animals. Many occasions spontaneously arise for sorting and classifying during exploratory play.

By age two, children begin to explore putting things in order according to a pattern. At first it is random, that is, they do not pay attention to size or shape. When playing with a stacking toy, for example, they likely put the pieces together any old way. By age five, the notion of ordering by size, that is, largest to smallest, becomes established. From putting things in order vertically as a tower, children will then create horizontal roads. They will also begin to organize by pattern and can match a simple pattern in which only one attribute is different, such as red cube, blue cube, red cube, blue cube. The earliest explorations of space involve learning that their own bodies take up space and how to negotiate when on the move, as seen when using a mobile walker.

In terms of exploring the relationship between matter and space, one of the earliest actions is emptying. Twelve-month-old Brianna has discovered drawers and can open and empty one with great enthusiasm. She does the same with the laundry basket.

The fifteen-month-old will spend long periods of time emptying a cupboard or a bookshelf or a pantry. She takes everything out and waits for someone to put it back so that she can do it all over again. Sometimes this tendency to empty leads to stressful situations, as when the toddler empties the milk on the floor or the soup on the high-chair shelf. Parents need to remember that this is not done in order to irritate them but because the child wants to know "what happens when".

In time children become interested in filling things up. They will stuff all of their toys into the wagon or all of Mommy's jewelry into a shopping bag. They are attracted to purses and anything that can be used to tote things around. These are examples of spontaneous exploration of space.

Research shows that children who play are more efficient problem solvers than those who are given a demonstration to follow. Play reduces the stress of trying to find a solution and therefore children proceed with less fear of failure and frustration. Through play children learn that there is more than one way to act, and this leads to the flexibility of thinking that is at the heart of problem solving. Play has been found to be more effective in training children how to problem solve than direct instruction techniques.

Interest in the connection between play and problem solving as well as the development of creativity has continued to be a source of interest. Creativity is, after all, the essence of pretend play. When playfulness is encouraged, a child will be receptive to creative thinking. The effects of play don't diminish with time, and studies have shown that there is a connection between early pretend play and effective problem solving in older children.

Children who rate high on a playfulness scale rate higher on tests for creativity than those who were not playful. There is also a reciprocal link between social problem solving and play in the preschool years. It has been noted that problem-solving skills appear to improve the level of pretend play, and pretend play improves problem-solving skills. What studies tell us is that play does contribute to higher levels of thinking that are necessary for academic success in school.

It has been found that pretend play is an important vehicle for the development of *symbolic thinking*. Symbolic thinking is the ability to use symbols to represent objects or ideas. The toddler cruises around the room on her pedal toy making *vroom* sounds to represent a car. She knows that the pedal toy is not the same thing as Mommy's car, but she pretends that it is. In this case she uses language (e.g., the made-up word *vroom*) to suggest that the car is moving. Between ages three and six, the child moves back and forth between the world-as-it-is and world she inhabits in her imagination. This is symbolic thinking, and it takes place with tremendous inventiveness during the early years.

By age five, symbolic thinking and imagination are well developed.

Five-year-old Lena is playing in the home center. She invites me to come for coffee.

"I'll call you," she says, handing me a toy telephone.

She then begins to search for the other toy telephone that seems to have vanished. After several moments of hunting for it, she exclaims, "Oh, never mind. I'll talk to you on the iron." At that she picks up the wooden iron, and a simulated telephone conversation takes place.

Symbolic thinking is the foundation for academic success in literacy, mathematics, and problem solving, as well as artistic representation. There could be no language without symbolic thought. Talk is the use of abstract words to represent real objects, people, and situations. Letters of the alphabet and words are symbols that represent ideas. The word ball is not an actual ball, but it represents the object so that when we read the word, we visualize a ball. These are not obvious benefits of play, but they are highly significant.

> *For an overview of play and development see Pretend Play and Young Children's Development by Doris Bergen (ERIC Digest, 2001).*

In addition to exploration and pretend play, games can offer an enjoyable means of extending the mental capacity in children. Games are a way to practice the emerging mathematical tools of sorting, putting things in order, counting, and recognizing spatial relations.

Play Develops Language

Learning language begins with listening, then comes talking, and finally literacy, that is reading and writing. These four systems are connected, although each has its own developmental characteristics. We need to remember that language and thinking go hand in hand: talking and writing express what is going on in the mind; listening and reading feed the mind.

Long before a child can talk, she is able to understand a great deal of language through listening. By the early stages of the toddler years, she responds to simple requests such as "bring me your bottle." She also responds to the language of songs and rhymes by smiling and bouncing. She is aware of different kinds of noises, distinguishes familiar voices, and is sensitive to the tone of voice.

The first oral communication is babbling. By around eight months, your baby's babbling includes nearly all of the sounds of her first language. She uses these sounds to communicate her needs and is quite sensitive to what you communicate to her through your tone of voice. She knows the difference between playful talk and anger.

Children learn to talk by talking and being talked to. The first words she speaks are always related to what is important to her. There is a predictable pattern to the way in which children learn to talk, although they do so at an individual pace. In general, the first words appear just before the age of twelve months. Vocabulary grows slowly, but toward the end of the second year, a growth spurt is likely to occur, and suddenly the child cannot get enough of words. They repeat everything they hear over and over, and they make up new ones as needed.

Some children are slow to begin to talk; others start well before their first birthday. Again this is a personal developmental pattern. Some children remain at the babbling stage for months; others move quickly into producing words and even phrases. This is natural and there is likely nothing to be concerned with.

I remember when Lisa was a toddler. At age two she was incredibly well coordinated, but she rarely attempted any speech. She obviously could understand what was said to her, but it was not until around twenty-eight-months that she began to speak. Overnight she spoke in complete sentences, using a well-developed vocabulary.

Children who are rapidly advancing in physical development may be slower to begin to talk. It seems that when one area of development is perking, the others go on the back burner for a while.

Parents should be concerned only if their child does not seem to understand or to hear what is being said. It is always wise to check with your pediatrician when language development is not moving as it ought, but generally, it is likely to be the child's individual timetable at work.

By the time a child is talking in sentences, she has already learned a great deal about language. She has acquired a vocabulary of words that grows with each new experience and opportunity to chat. She has learned about the turn-taking nature of conversation, and she has picked up on the use of pitch, tone of voice, and the rhythm of the phrase. We have only to listen to our children as they play house to hear our own voices with the inflection and tone of the occasion. It serves to remind us that young children absorb much more than we could ever imagine, including our black moods and our frustrations.

> *Experts tell us that within six months to one year after beginning to speak in sentences, children will have mastered the basic grammar of their native language. They go through a pattern of producing sentences that is beyond imitation as they make two-word "sentences," then three-word "sentences," and then full sentences. This is an amazing achievement.*

Reading is a complicated process requiring an appropriate level of mental and language readiness. Mental readiness means that a child has developed fundamental symbolic thinking, such as the fact that one object can represent another. A block is not a car, but she can pretend that it is. From understanding the use of one object as a symbol of another she needs to understand the use of letters and words to represent ideas.

Reading is built on oral language and what is called a *meta-cognitive* understanding of grammar. This means that although she cannot talk about grammar and sentences and other aspects of language, she is amazingly accurate in using the correct part of speech and shows her understanding of the natural breaks in sentences as she play reads out loud. This is why experts in second language learning tell us that it is extremely important for children to have a well-developed first language. Children who have a well-established first language will pick up a second quite readily when they are in a situation where they need to use it.

The first time I met Ora, a beautiful two-year-old Thai child, she spoke no English. Her mom and I were doctoral candidates together and had become friends. Ora spent a year in Toronto, and each time I saw her it was clear that her English was developing rapidly, although she preferred to have her mom speak to her in Thai. A year later, at age three, when she was returning home to Bangkok, she spoke and sang in English better than many of her peers at the daycare center. A second language is easy for a young child when there is a genuine need to learn it.

We don't often think about the physical readiness for reading, but this can be an important factor. The eye muscles, for example, need to be sufficiently developed to allow a young child to focus on the print.

Although there has been a flurry of research over the past several decades investigating how children learn to write, this process remains largely misunderstood by society at large. From the work of Donald Graves (1983), Lucy Calkins (1986), and others, we know that like reading, learning to write follows predictable stages of development and that the process begins in the early years. Just as there is a pretalk stage of babbling and a prereading stage of reading, so too there is *prewriting stage of scribbling.* It was long thought that the scribbles of young children were just that, with no meaning or significance. We now know, however, that this is a vital step toward becoming a writer.

Invented spelling is a transition between the scribble stage and conventional writing and continues on through the primary grades. Invented spelling is done when a child writes down the letters she hears. For example, pajamas may appear as *pjmz* and eyes is likely to be *iz*. At the beginning of this stage, few vowels appear because they are not clearly distinguishable to a child. Over time young writers are able to accept spelling instruction without it limiting the creative nature of written language.

How Play Supports Language Learning

Play is a powerful means of developing every aspect of language. This includes the following:

- developing vocabulary to include an increasingly extensive use of descriptive words,

- refining conventional speech in the use of such things as the correct use of verb tenses, and

- expanding the uses of language as a means of voicing imagination, negotiating conflicts, and directing the actions of others.

Exploratory play provides a serious boost to the growth of vocabulary as young children try to describe what they see and do.

Several children were playing at the water table, experimenting with things that could float and those that sank.

At one point I asked, "How could we get this boat to sink?"

"Push it very down," said Mark.

"We could push it down," I said, "but how will we get it to stay?"

"Make it big," said Mark.

I put an additional piece on the boat, but it still floated back up.

"Not like that," he said, as he placed a heavy stone on top of it.

Mark had no word for heavy, although he knew the concept. This experience added a new word to his vocabulary that he used over and over during the next few weeks as he played at the water table.

Exploratory play such as this provides countless opportunities for giving directions and following directions. The descriptive language so vital to both science and math is generated as children talk about their explorations.

The strongest motivation for language learning is social. At any age, humans have a profound need to connect with others. Nowhere is the connection between language and social development more visible than in pretend play. Indeed, language is one of the four essential components of sociodramatic play. As a social activity, sociodramatic play offers real and meaningful opportunities to cooperate, collaborate, communicate, and negotiate. It is by far a more powerful way to teach children how to get along with one another than any contrived set of prepackaged lessons.

Pretend play has a direct role in developing early reading. The most advanced players in sociodramatic play are those who have the most advanced language and social skills. It is these children who can set up an episode, negotiate the action plan, and resolve conflicts. These are likely to be the superior readers as well, although not necessarily the earliest to begin. Sociodramatic play equips children for reading and writing by providing the opportunity to develop important skills basic to reading for understanding. These include the following:

- creating characters;

- creating a series of related events;

- expanding their vocabulary as they play different roles and situations;

- helping them understand how language is used to express emotions and ideas, as well as give to information and instructions;

- listening for details;

- following directions;

- telling the difference between the sounds of the letters and words (auditory discrimination);

- noticing the difference between the letters of the alphabet as well as other aspects, such as the order of the letters in a word, the use of uppercase letters, and so on; and

- developing memory and attentive behavior.

From exploring the uses of written language to the expansion of vocabulary and perspective taking, children who play learn to read and write much more easily than those who do not.

What Can We Do To Help?

Play addresses all of a child's developmental needs in an integrated way. A child's development is not chopped up into separate areas and addressed through a series of directed lessons. It is the ordinary, everyday play that provides the extraordinary growth and development of the mind, the body, and the spirit of a young child.

Development of the Body

➢ Health is surely one of the most valuable gifts we give our children. It is never too early to introduce physical activity through play. Play supports development of every aspect of physical growth, and it does so according to the needs of the individual child. Children are quite remarkable in their ability to select activities that move them ahead developmentally without compromising their safety. This doesn't mean they won't have a tumble or hurt themselves on a slide. It means that in the regular course of events, children tend to find their own limits.

➢ Lifelong habits begin in the early years. Children who learn to enjoy nutritious snacks will be adults who enjoy healthy eating. Children who learn to love getting outdoors to play are not likely to be adults who spend their leisure munching on chips and watching television.

➢ Large muscle development precedes fine muscle development. For this reason, children under the age of four should be provided with a wide variety of equipment used to strengthen their motor development. This means regular time at an outdoor playground as well as ride-on toys, balls, and other standard equipment.

Development of the Mind

➢ Play stimulates brain activity in a powerful way. It allows children to learn things that could never be taught through direct instruction. Capitalizing on the vigorous growth of the brain in the first years of life does not require that we stuff children with facts and skills at the expense of the deep significant development and learning taking place through play.

➢ There's more to math than counting. Provide blocks or items such as buttons, shells, and beads for sorting and counting. Make it possible for your children to explore seriation and patterning through stacking toys and a variety of types of puzzles.

➢ For some children language may precede understanding of notions fundamental to math and science. Don't be fooled into expecting your child to do math operations before she understands the notion of conservation (four is four whether it is four huge tractors or four tiny chicks).

Development of Language

➢ Learning to read and to write follow learning to talk. A child who has a rich vocabulary and has mastered more or less the basics of sentence structure by age six is likely to begin to read independently, but there is no fixed time when a child should begin to either talk or read.

> It is important to remember that a well-established first language is basic to learning to read. Sometimes immigrant parents worry that their child will not succeed if they speak in their own first language to her. It seems that if a five-year-old is fluent in his family's first language, then he will quickly pick up the language spoken at school.

> Early reading should be a source of pleasure without undue stress or frustration on the part of the child, and for that matter, the parent. For a while after the child begins to read, she will move in and out of interest. This is not cause for concern but simply an indication of how the developmental energy is working. Reading is only one aspect of important development for the young child. The key thing is to respect the child's individual timetable and remain confident that in time she will read.

The body and the mind do not develop in isolation from one another. Each has a profound influence on the other. A child who is malnourished, tired, or physically confined will have his mental abilities curtailed. Children need their play in order for the development of the body and mind to be integrated and flourish.

For suggestions see Part 4 Resources: Toys and Activities that Develop the Body and the Mind.

A little glitter and a collection of natural materials can become a work of art.

5

Learning through Play: The Self and the Artist

The child starts off as an artist with a mind of his own. He is equipped to become the architect of his own personality and ultimate destiny. Each child by nature sets off in the right direction.

Alice Yardley

Did you know that self-esteem is a better predictor of academic success than IQ? Positive self-esteem comes about by being confident and competent. Self-esteem provides a sense of well-being and security that allow a child to be a risk-taker. Nurturing self-confidence is a major contribution to your child's future success.

Play Develops a Positive Sense of Self

When we talk about nurturing self-esteem, we are not talking simply about the "warm fuzzies," where everything receives praise even when it does not warrant it. Self-esteem is a genuine, deep sense of self-worth that is the bedrock of learning. This means that we provide genuine praise for accomplishments and help our child learn how to accept failure as part of learning. We do this naturally when we accept the hesitant first steps or the earliest attempts at speech. As our child grows, we need to continue celebrating success and helping her see that failure is simply part of success. This helps children to realize that we all have different strengths and weaknesses and to appreciate our own individual talents.

There is a strong link between self-esteem and social development. How we feel about ourselves is reflected back to us from those around us, that is, our family and friends. They let us know that we have value from their reaction to our behavior. Babies begin to feel good about themselves when they are surrounded by those who love them. As each smile, tear, and gesture the baby makes is welcomed with approval and delight, a baby begins to feel that he is worthwhile. As the months pass by and each new accomplishment is celebrated, confidence grows and new challenges are met. Competence first in sitting up, then in crawling, and finally teetering along on her own two feet gives an infant the satisfaction and assurance that she can master her world.

As children grow, friends play an increasingly important role in developing healthy self-esteem. By the late middle years, the opinion of friends becomes more important than that of the family. Good relationships with friends are necessary for healthy social development. Good friendships require the ability to listen to others, feel empathy, and put our own needs aside when it is necessary to help our friends.

The social network of friendship has a tremendous power to influence a child's behavior in both good ways and bad. Even in the early years, a child can be influenced to do unacceptable things by an overbearing friend. This kind of relationship erodes self-esteem and may lay the groundwork for serious social and mental-health problems later on in life.

For most children, developing the skills to forge and maintain close relationships is a positive experience. Today's children are often exposed to social settings outside of their home at an early age. Some infants as young as five months attend childcare. Although every attempt is made in good childcare facilities to provide personal attention, the fact remains that there are competing needs among the babies that go well beyond what would be expected in a home. Ideally, parents may have the luxury of placing their young child in a preschool or childcare on a part-time basis. This provides the opportunity for young children to adjust to the needs of other children and to the changes in expectation. Within a short time, toddlers pick up on the fact that there are differences in what is accepted at home and what is expected at the center.

Social Development through Play

Traditionally, the play of babies and toddlers was referred to as solitary play. This term conveyed the fact that very young children cannot participate in the give and take of a social experience. Babies were thought to be too self-absorbed to need play partners. Right from the beginning, however, play is social. Although a baby functions on instinct and self-gratification, he needs the company of other people to stimulate his play. Children can certainly play by themselves, but having others there to share in the experience adds richness.

The classic description of the social patterns in the development of play comes from the work of Mildred Parten (1933). Parten set out a framework for what has been the most common way of talking about stages of social development in play. She identified six stages, those being unoccupied, solitary, onlooker, parallel, associative, and cooperative. This provided a useful starting point for observation, but I believe through the work of Vygotsky and others who have recognized the social nature of play that these terms are no longer as relevant. While babies may not be able to enter into a give-and-take type of play, they want those around them to join in. For this reason I prefer to call this personal play rather than solitary play.

I watched eleven-month-old Brianna playing with an empty plastic water bottle. After biting on it, squeezing it, and banging on a chair with it, she began to drop it on the floor. Her aunt Lorna picked it up and gave it back to her. She kept dropping it, giggling each time as her aunt picked it up once again.

This story illustrates the personal nature of play. The play partner, in this case Brianna's aunt Lorna, is more or less a prop for Brianna's play. Brianna initiates the actions and keeps it going as long as she is interested and her aunt is willing.

Moving into the toddler years, children play with one another but still in a self-absorbed personal way, although now there is *cooperation*. As toddlers mature, the cooperation increases and we often find that they play the same theme, although their actions remain personal. Three-year-old Clare and her friend Micah attend preschool together. They get out the dolls and play house, feeding and burping the dolls. There is no attempt to imitate a family; they just share the play itself.

There will be times when a child is an onlooker or when two or more children prefer to play side by side, but there remains the quality of a social occasion. The cooperative phase provides a transition into collaborative play, in which there is a common goal and the children work together to sustain their play.

By age five, children become increasingly involved with one another, and eventually *collaborative play* is born. Now children share in common activities as they play dress-up or build a sandcastle. Each player has a part to play, and the collaboration needed to make the play work requires mature language and social skills. If a less mature child joins and does not keep to the authenticity of the theme, the others will quickly eject that child. Play is the best place for children to learn the give and take of getting along with others.

Learning how to get along in society begins with learning how to get along with your brother.

Chart 5.1

SOCIAL PATTERNS IN EARLY PLAY	
Forms	**Characteristics**
Personal Play	• Traditionally referred to as solitary play • Infant and toddler likes company of others while playing but play follows his own purposes • Not able to work together with another • Shows high level of concentration and absorption
Cooperative Play	• Play side by side and chat • Share toys and space but follows own agenda • Sometimes acts as an onlooker
Collaborative Play	• Begins at age 4 and continues • Shares toys and space and works together on building a shared product • First seen in use of blocks – children make a car out of several blocks and pretend to go for a ride • At first will involve two children • First collaborative partners are children who know one another well. Only later will they begin to include new-comers

Play has a vital role in developing self-esteem. It is often by a parent playfully responding to the baby's attempts at mastery of physical skills that he gains confidence to meet new challenges and overcome frustration at his limitations. In play, failure is not taken seriously. Watch as a baby tries to stand. He barely makes it, and then plunks down on his bottom. The parent is teasing and making up funny noises to encourage him to continue. We cannot imagine any parent standing by as the baby tries to stand, scolding him for not succeeding, although later on when he starts school we will do this with any number of new attempts at learning. There is nothing more wrenching than seeing a five-year-old who has given up on himself because he doesn't measure up to what is expected.

Play is the forum for learning the social skills of

- self-control,

- acceptable behavior,

- group participation, and

- cultivating friendships

Play, and in particular sociodramatic play, provides a unique experience in learning how to establish and sustain relationships. This requires the skills of turn taking, perspective taking (that is, seeing things from the point of view of another person), and finding positive ways of dealing with conflict. It is a real milestone of social development when a young child can use language to express feelings of disapproval.

Lucas is trying to put a puzzle together. Ora wants him to play at the home center with her. When he ignores her requests, she grabs pieces of the puzzle and refuses to give them back. In exasperation, Lucas says, "I don't like you what you're up to!" A few months earlier, Lucas would have used physical aggression to retrieve the pieces, but now he attempts to use language.

As children try to develop and sustain a shared make-believe episode, things don't always go smoothly. Arguments arise. Who is going to take which part? What props will each use? How will the story unfold? Each aspect of the episode must be worked out if it is to be successful. In her study *Socio-dramatic Play: A Context for Conflict Resolution* (1996), Ruth Magnusdottir found that conflict during play served as a positive stimulus to negotiation and problem solving. She saw the positive benefits of conflict as a reflection on the fact that in sociodramatic play, children can control their own affairs. When allowed to do so, they learn to use language rather than physical means to resolve problems. In play, conflict is not negative but rather a means of learning how to

- negotiate and share power,

- explore acceptable ways of behaving,

- resolve conflict without resorting to violence, and

- strengthen and maintain the play community.

All of these social skills require a high level of communication. Sociodramatic play stretches language from simple uses such as naming objects, asking questions, and requesting things to the much higher uses of expressing feelings, discussing options, and formulating arguments. These are essential skills for social interaction. No other activity of childhood provides these experiences as powerfully as does play. Play offers a safe place to argue, to express feelings, and so on. Children actually develop some sophisticated strategies to use when things break down. Such phrases as "you can't play" are brought to bear. What this seems to do is offer a way of getting out of a power struggle while maintaining the play. It has been my experience that seldom does the expelled child actually leave the group. He is likely to drop out of role momentarily and then resume his role as if nothing happened.

Sociodramatic play provides the opportunity for children to deal with the issues of inclusion and exclusion. They learn that unacceptable behavior, whether aggressive or inappropriate, will result in their being ejected from the play. Similarly, they learn that if they do not share the toys and props of play, they will not be invited to join. Sociodramatic play offers a safe place in which to learn the valuable lessons of how to get along with others.

Play provides a unique experience for children of what it means to be part of a community. There are rules that govern communal play and children intuitively know what they are.

- They must use authentic actions and language.

- They must stay in character.

- They must share the roles and toys.

- They must agree on the direction of the story.

At the heart of all of these rules is the ability to collaborate with others. Children need to cooperate in many situations as they share toys and space with siblings and peers. Collaboration, however, goes much further. For collaboration to take place, there must be a common goal and a shared story. An episode of make-believe play provides a powerful forum for the development of collaboration. Collaboration is considered to be one of the most important skills in the marketplace of today. There is no better way to begin the development of these skills than through play.

*Children who learn to play well on their own will
be children who play well with others.*

Chart 5.2

PARENT-CHILD RELATIONSHIPS	
Supporting Self-Esteem	
Four Sure-fire Ingredients	**What Can We Do?**
1. Find out what really matters to your child	• Respect your child's interests and needs. Achievement that increases self-esteem will be based on how much the child cares about the success. If we push our children to succeed at something we wanted to do ourselves, no matter how successful, it will not bring satisfaction or a sense of personal worth.
2. Provide emotional support and social approval	• Express affection particularly in the face of disappointment. Children are generally their own worst critics. They know when they fail and the last thing they want is to let their parents down.
3. Help your child learn to cope with set-backs and failure	• Take your child's problems seriously. In the grand scheme of things it may be trivial, but to a child it may be devastating
4. Build on her strengths	• Set clear and fair rules and then stick to them. Children need to know the limits! • Allow enough freedom for risk-taking and allowance for failure

Getting along with others is not a trivial skill but the mainstay of healthy relationships in one's personal life as well as one's workplace. We have all known people who were talented and smart but who could not achieve their potential because of their poor interpersonal skills. This may be a far cry from physically violent individuals, but it all comes from poor socialization in the early years. There are, of course, many factors both from nature and nurturing that contribute to aggression and antisocialism, but one thing is clear: children who play well in the early years are far more likely to be happy, successful individuals in later life.

Play Develops Artistic Ability

Children's play is filled with song and dance, with color and design. It is the best possible way for children to explore their inner artistic selves. In play, there is no one right way to dance or to paint. It is under the child's control.

The arts are widely recognized as a critical ingredient for development and learning. The link between language and the arts is a natural one, with both providing a means of communication. Studies have shown that music and mathematics involve similar brain activities and that the musician and the mathematician have common ways of thinking. Experiencing music through both listening and participating will provide a rich resource for much growth and learning not only in music but also in all areas of development.

Music and dance provide the child with

- a powerful means of expressing feelings,

- an enjoyable social activity that promotes cooperation and positive interaction, and

- an opportunity to control body movement and develop grace.

From infancy, children learn the effective power of music to soothe and comfort. Music can also help a child to

- develop humor,

- develop a love of language and music, and

- become aware of, and appreciate, the richness of unfamiliar cultures and traditions.

The visual arts are linked to important learning outcomes. Painting and making three-dimensional models provide another type of artistic expression for the young child. From the nine-month-old painting the highchair tray with pureed peas to the toddler making sweeping strokes across the wall with lipstick, parents are well aware that young children find great satisfaction in expressing themselves with any medium they find.

The timeless fascination that children have with play dough and other squishy materials speaks to the need for tactile experiences in the early years. Although there may seem to be little pattern or design in these early pieces, there is a primitive symbolism that is quite remarkable.

The arts promote

- creativity,

- aesthetic appreciation,

- self-expression,

- observation and descriptive language,

- self-confidence,

- mastery of everyday tools (e.g., scissors, paintbrush, pencil, and crayons), and

- skills in using a variety of materials (e.g., paints, clay, wood, cloth, and wool)

Children are naturally creative. They invent language, they build structures, and they make up exquisite dances and chants, all as a result of their self-directed creative impulse. I have long wondered at the disappearance of this carefree creativity in children in the middle years. What happens to destroy creativity so quickly? Some of this behavior can be attributed to developmental changes in the children themselves. By the middle years, children become increasingly self-conscious. They also recognize the limitations of their skills with respect to producing quality art. Indeed, children of this age are their own strongest critics.

The decline of creativity in artistic expression can also be traced in large measure to the inappropriate but strongly rooted practices of crafts in the early years. In preschool and kindergarten, there is a long-standing tradition of teacher-directed crafts that serve to teach children from the earliest age to follow rigid ideas and a prescribed approach to art. This is where the notion of only one right way to do something begins. It is also the beginning of the focus on the end product rather than the process of self-expression.

Allowing child to be self-directed in the arts does not mean that they do not need assistance with techniques. Showing children how to do something and how to use materials wisely does not have to detract from the self-directed nature of artistic expression. It is when and how we provide instruction that matters. There can be a great deal of skill in some crafts, and as with playing instruments, you cannot be creative if you do not have the technical skills. Like so many things, we need to remember that the early years are best spent learning spontaneously through play and that technical skill can be taught after the child has ample opportunity to explore the materials and the processes.

In his classic book, *The Arts and Human Development* (1994), Howard Gardner explores the connections between the arts and play and the profound influence of both on child development. He argues that "art is a goal directed form of play." He states:

> Play is a foundation for all types of artistic expression, stimulating the imagination and nurturing the creative capacity. As children dance and twirl in their play, they are developing the physical coordination needed for more formalized dance. As they pound and squish play dough, they are beginning to develop

the fine muscles needed to be a sculptor. Thus, in
every sense, play is art.

To play is to imagine. To some extent all forms of play rely on
imagination, even games with rules, at least in the early stages. Later
on we need imagination in such things as a game of bridge as we try
to make the best bids. Children use imagination as they experiment
through exploratory play. While pretend play involves some imitation
of what children know from everyday life, imagination is needed
to rework these bits and pieces of experience into new stories.
Imagination can never rest while a child is at play.

Long before children can put words to them, play offers a concrete
way to express deeply felt emotions as well as originality. Play,
particularly make-believe, allows children to get beyond inhibitions
and the limits of self-consciousness. This liberation enables children
to approach the arts with confidence. From the play experiences,
children not only believe in their own ideas but they know that what
they do has value.

It is quite common to see young children singing softly as they rock
their dollies to sleep. They demonstrate that they understand the
soothing quality of music. Similarly, they enter into a rousing march
as they play out a wedding scene or simply sing a favorite tune to
themselves as they play with a puzzle. We see them using play dough
to shape food for the table or cookies for the oven. They use their
visual art to make props for the sociodramatic play or to decorate a
sandcastle.

As with all aspects of development, children do not segment knowledge
into compartments as we do with most areas of the curriculum.
To children, the arts are one of a piece, each contributing to self-
expression.

*I was visiting some children in one of my favorite junior kindergarten
classrooms when I noticed two boys playing at the sand table. As I
watched, one little boy said, "We're building a castle."*

"Who lives in it?" I asked.

"A giant."

"Who else?" I asked.

"He's by himself."

"What's he having for dinner?" I asked.

"I dunno."

The boys continue to build and suddenly one of the boys said, "I know. Baloney tarts and tea!"

This caught the fancy of the other boy who began to chant "baloney tarts and tea." By now they had begun to skip around the sand table, and several other children joined in. Before long most of the class was skipping around the room in a long line chanting, "baloney tarts and tea."

This is a delightful example of how music, dance, and drama and even visual arts come together in an original composition.

In play children express their inner reality time and again, yet it goes largely unnoticed by the adults in their world. How rich our culture would be if this magnificent artistic power was nurtured and continued to flourish into adulthood. How many of us would be painters or musicians or dancers?

What Can We Do to Help?

Development of Self-Esteem and Social Skill

Every child deserves to have a parent who thinks she is the most wonderful baby ever born. Strengthen her sense of self-worth through genuine affirmation.

➤ Provide opportunities to place your young children in social situations that broaden their experience. Play groups for babies and toddlers make a good transition between home and preschool. Experts believe that if healthy socialization and positive self-esteem are not developed during these early years, they cannot be made up for later on. By the time the child reaches adolescence, the lessons of play may be lost forever.

➤ Remember that all areas of development progress in predictable stages but according to the individual timetable of the child. When one area is perking ahead, the others are likely to be on the back burner.

Development of Artistic Expression

➤ Surround children with music of all types. Dance and sing with them as you might during pregnancy. Music can provide tremendous stimulation for movement and dance, but it can also offer serenity in the midst of a hectic day. Children should experience the many moods of music from an early age. Provide musical instruments for experimentation and making rudimentary music.

➤ Make props and costumes available for pretend play that will spark themes of interest to the children. Make a prop box with interesting items for play and open-ended materials that can be used to create props and costumes. Play in role with the children, always letting them take the lead. You're not likely to be assigned the role of the baby or the dog—that is reserved for the younger players—but you won't be given the boss part either.

➤ Have an artist's kit available that can be moved as needed. The "kit" could be a dishpan or a caddy for cleaning products. Plastic bottles, cans, and other containers that fit into the compartments can hold paints, brushes, markers, glue, scissors, and other tools. A storage box can be used for paper, cloth, and other materials.

When we observe a young child, we see that he is creative and imaginative and at heart an artist. He has a natural urge to make his mark on the world, and unless he is discouraged from doing so, he experiments with many kinds of materials. For a child, art is not restricted to music and dance and painting, but encompasses his exploration of language and mathematics. Technology becomes a tool for artistic expression. The arts provide a child with a unique means of understanding himself and sharing his self-expression with others. In this sense, art is at once intensely personal and exquisitely social.

Part 2

Making It Happen

The merging of the neuroscience story with the developmental story has increased our understanding of how fundamental the first years of a child's life are in laying the base for the future. We are beginning to understand the linkage between the way the brain develops, and the neurological and biological pathways that affect learning, behaviour and health through out life.
Margaret McCain and Fraser Mustard

6

The Playscape

"The first years last forever" is much more than a slogan. Research in Canada and around the world clearly shows that our health, well-being and coping skills in adulthood and old age are strongly influenced by our start in life...

We know that children need a responsive and interactive environment of talking and reading, mentoring and encouragement of exploration through play, warmth and acceptance, and protection from teasing and punishment.

Clyde Hertzman

There are many things that we as parents and teachers can do to ensure that play has priority of place in our children's lives. Supporting learning through play begins with the playscape. This involves finding time and a place as well as the toys and materials needed. We must also find time to enjoy play with our children. There are many valuable ways in which we can extend and enrich children's play through our thoughtful participation.

A Time and a Place to Play

Children need sufficient stretches of time to develop and carry out their play. One of the main causes of the lack of time for children to play is over-scheduling too many organized activities. In our society, children have become as harried as parents. They scurry from one activity to another with scarcely breathing room between. Experts believe that placing children in too many organized activities and lessons is not healthy and certainly cuts into time for play. Parents must remember that what children learn through play should be a priority. There is nothing wrong with lessons and organized activities, provided that they are developmentally appropriate and selected with the needs and interest of the child in mind.

Sometimes parents enroll their children in sports or the arts because they missed out on these things themselves. Not a good motive! We need to step back and assess what's happening. A limit to the number of lessons and outside activities can be established with time left for family activities as well as for spontaneous play.

Computer games and television have their place but not as a substitute for play. Like adults, children too need to have the kind of escape that television or video games can provide, but when this takes over from play, a good deal of important learning is lost. For the most part, media offers little opportunity for collaboration and play. Although things are changing rapidly in the production of video games and television programs for very young children, many of them still tend to be limited in what they require of the mind. Children's television programs have improved greatly in the past few years, but for all of that, TV and video cannot replace play as a premier means of growth and development.

After a day filled with hassles, it may be easier when we arrive home late and have to prepare dinner to put our children in front of the TV than to encourage play. This is bound to happen, but we have to be careful that the TV does not become a permanent babysitter.

Families today are pulled in many directions as we try to balance scheduled activities for our children with work demands, upkeep of the home, and our own needs for exercise and relaxation. Many children live with a single parent or have both parents working. Remember that so long as parents are available, children can be self-directed for quite some time. This allows children to control their own play without interference from adults.

There should, however, be times when we as parents become actively involved in our child's play. Being a play partner begins in the early playfulness we have with our infant. It continues in all the ways we enjoy playing with them, from roughhousing to pretending, from singing and dancing to a card game.

For parents, finding time to join in our children's play can be quite a challenge. Recognizing the importance of connecting with their children, some busy parents prefer to spend what has come to be called "quality time." It has been my experience that for some parents this means that when they can manage it, they will spend a designated amount of time with the child usually doing something of the parents' choosing.

It seems to me that most often when a parent is ready to provide quality time, the child is not interested. A young child simply wants to know that her parent is there and will, if needed, get involved.

While out walking in my neighborhood late one fall afternoon, I came upon two little girls under five years of age playing in a huge pile of leaves. The mom sat on the steps watching as they leapt and sang and threw leaves everywhere. As I stopped to speak to her, the mom commented, "I should be in cooking supper by now, but they are having way too much fun. I think this is the night to open a can of soup and make cheese sandwiches."

How wise! There's a whole long winter ahead during which to make hearty home-cooked meals, but the beauty of a glorious fall afternoon is fleeting. This is an example of being involved without interfering in the play. The mom was able to sit back and delight in what her children were doing. She showed her positive feelings toward play, encouraged them to cooperate, and was able to relax at the same time. When a squabble broke out over sharing equipment, the mom encouraged them to share the rake and take turns. Although the mom was not actively playing in the leaves with them, the girls were secure and felt safe knowing she was there.

Play places are becoming hard to find. When adults revisit their memories of childhood play, we remember fondly a favorite place that was an "adult-free zone." Attics and cellars were once treasured play spaces, but these have all but disappeared from our homes. I remember one time I was conducting a workshop with school administrators, and as we shared our memories of play, one school director told us about growing up in a small overcrowded cottage in

Ireland. As one of many children, privacy was difficult to come by, but he had a space behind his grandfather's huge, old armchair. No one else was allowed back there, and he spent many hours playing with his toys in the security of his grandfather's shadow. So powerful was this memory that the telling brought tears to his eyes.

Finding a place to play is a major concern for the many urban parents who live in dense housing complexes. Parents worry about letting their young children play outdoors or go to a nearby park, even with older siblings. Their living quarters may be too cramped to allow children a play space.

A community outreach worker that I knew told me the story of one family whom she visited. Two adults and four young children were living in two rooms above a store in a busy downtown neighborhood. To make a playhouse in the midst of this crowded space, the mom put a blanket over the kitchen table and added a cardboard box with various pieces of clothing and found materials, such as empty plastic containers and tinfoil. It was amazing what the children did with this space. When mealtime came, of course, it was easily restored to a dining table.

Parents do not have to face these challenges alone. At the suggestion of the outreach worker, the mom in the previous story began to take her children to various community centers, such as the local library and a parent drop-in center located in a nearby school. This particular mother had the added benefit of finding several other mothers who lived near her apartment, and they formed a support group for one another. It takes ingenuity, but there is always the possibility of a solution.

Schools today are experiencing many of the same challenges to play that parents face. Where once it was assumed that children played in preschool and kindergarten, increasingly this is becoming a thing of the past. Finding time and enough space for play in preschools and kindergartens has its own set of challenges. For play to have maximum benefits, children need a sustained period of time, no less than one hour per half day. This should not be difficult to achieve in preschool, but in kindergarten the time for play is often disrupted for other school priorities. While each has value, these should not be more important than play, nor should they be allowed to erode the time children need for play. If we believe in the value of play, we can find ways of organizing the space and time so that play is not the first thing to go!

Having adequate space to get the maximum benefit from play is not easy in kindergarten classrooms. Cramped spaces, added to overcrowding, along with inappropriate expectations, have eroded what was once the happiest of learning places. There was a time when a kindergarten classroom was given priority in schools. The kindergarten classroom was often the largest room in the school with child-size washrooms attached. Large windows and colorful equipment such as large wooden blocks, climbers, and other gross-motor-skills equipment were considered standard necessities. A piano and set of good-quality rhythm instruments would be found in every kindergarten classroom. To teach kindergarten, teachers needed the standard elementary teacher qualifications, but in addition, they were required to study early childhood and be qualified in piano.

Today within regular school systems, rooms allocated for kindergarten are often intended for a traditional elementary class. Cupboards and other fixed features in these classrooms are too high and inaccessible to small children. This makes it difficult to set up routines or have supplies and equipment readily available for children to access.

Sometimes in both kindergartens and daycare centers there is too much inflexible, heavy furniture. Tables and chairs are provided for every child, even though it is rare that all children sit down at the same time. Whole group experiences such as story time are usually held in a circle with children sitting on a carpet.

I recall a conversation I had with a junior kindergarten teacher regarding space for play. The room was a standard-size elementary classroom with twenty-five four-year-olds in the room. The tables and chairs took up most of the floor space. The teacher came up with several suggestions for freeing up more space, beginning by removing some of the tables and chairs. It turned out that the only time they were used by all children at the same time was for snack. There were a number of possible ways of changing this routine, including allowing children to have a snack when they were hungry, rather than when they were told to. In the end, she traded some of her tables and chairs with other teachers in exchange for a movable shelving unit. She placed a remnant of carpet and some fluffy pillows in an area where children could go to look at picture books and read. The reorganizing made the room hum more smoothly with less bickering caused by overcrowding.

Just because traditionally things have been done in a certain way does not mean it must always be so. We need to rethink how we use a child's time to make the most out of the school experience. It is not by accident that when asked what do you like best at school, many young children as early as grade one will respond, "gym and recess."

If as a teacher you find yourself in an overcrowded, poorly equipped room, there are ways to alleviate the situation. To begin with, you need to step back and do an inventory of the furniture and equipment in the room:

- What is being well used?

- What is used only on a limited basis?

- What is getting in the way?

- What is missing?

- How well is the storage space organized?

- Are there areas within the school/outdoors that could be used more effectively for play?

Once the inventory has been completed, you can discuss the situation with the principal and other staff members for a possible exchange of items. When budget time rolls around, prepare a list of items with a rationale that can be used by your administrator to make decisions about materials and equipment. You are the one who knows what is needed. Remind her that toys are your textbooks.

You then need to remove unnecessary tables and chairs. Do you really need a chair for every child? How often do they all sit around tables at once? By adding pillows, carpets, and other things to sit on, such as a comfortable rocking chair or a small loveseat, you will gain flexibility in the use of space.

Next you need to check to see if there is any additional space outside your classroom that could be of use. I've seen a number of situations where the kindergarten and primary classes used hallways.

One grade-two class wanted to set up a theme mall, but they found that they couldn't fit it into their existing classroom. They wrote a letter to the principal requesting permission to set it up in the hall outside their classroom. This was a dead-end space with no traffic flow. It turned out to be ideal for this purpose. The mall was such a success that other classes wanted to join in, and soon a school-wide project was under way.

This may not be ideal for younger children, but using a space such as this as a parking garage for ride-on toys alleviates congestion, making more room for play.

Toys and Materials: The Stuff of Play

Toys are the textbooks of early learning. All toys can be educational. The toys and materials used in play serve both to suggest what the child will play and offer a means for imitating and imagining worlds of possibility.

As children grow, toy preferences change. What attracts a five-month-old is different from what attracts a five-year-old. Some toys are attractive at any age, but the way in which a child plays with a toy depends upon his stage of development. If we watch how children play with dolls, for example, we see that the infant simply cuddles the doll, whereas the three-year-old "mothers" the baby, feeding it, tucking it into bed, and so on. If we watch a fourteen-month-old child play with a stacking toy, we see that he places the pieces randomly, but at age three we will see him deliberately place the pieces in order of size. He may still play with the same toy, but now his purpose is different. This is why there is no one right way to play.

*A stick can be a weapon, a magic wand, a baton,
or anything else the child imagines it to be.*

Toys have changed a lot in this age of technology. The over-stimulation is incredible. Everything has to beep and flash and bob up and down but, as Andrea Gordon (2007) says in a newspaper article, "Simple

Fun," a small but growing group of toy makers and parents are harkening back to a time when toys were more about the wonder of kids than the wonder of technology.

Some toys stand the test of time and culture. Dolls, for example, have been an important part of children's play across the centuries. I am not talking about one of those expensive, sexy dolls on the shelves today, but basic dolls that little children can cuddle and dress up and mother.

Some toys are structured with a specific use in mind. Examples of structured toys would be puzzles, board games, and replicas, such as a toy village or a miniature dollhouse. Toys and costumes that have a distinct theme, such as construction vehicles, a firefighter's hat, or a baker's apron, can suggest a theme for pretend play, although children are wonderfully versatile in how they use toys and materials. If left alone to be creative, they can adapt almost anything to their play needs.

The best toys and materials for pretend play are those that are multipurpose, unstructured, and open-ended. Materials such as clay; scraps of wood; blocks of all shapes, sizes, and material; and lengths of cloth are flexible and stir a child's imagination. A stick can be anything from a hobbyhorse to a magic wand. Similarly, there are open-ended materials that allow a child to create props and costumes to fit the play. A scarf or a large piece of cloth can become Superman's cloak or a cover for the baby doll. Play dough can be made into endless objects to enhance an episode of dramatic play.

Mrs. Hewitt's mother was getting rid of a collection of small, lacy tablecloths suitable for card tables. She brought these into the classroom, thinking to use them to decorate a display table. Before she could put them to use, the children discovered them, and before long a wedding with four brides was in full swing. With the cloths draped over their heads, the girls announced that the teacher and I were invited to the wedding. We had to buy our tickets, we were lead to the sofa in the home center, and the brides marched in to a rendition of Jingle Bells.

This amazing wedding was repeated at least five times with more and more children joining, including two boys becoming brides. What a wonderful use of outdated tablecloths.

Parents and teachers sometimes tell me that they feel that they don't have the imagination to become involved in play. My advice is to follow the lead set by the children, and they will draw you in. If they need something to use as a prop, encourage them to improvise. You will be delighted with the outcome.

Many of the toys and materials preferred by young children are quite simple. We all have seen the child open up an expensive toy, put it aside after a few minutes, and then spend endless hours playing with the empty box. An imaginative preschool teacher tells this story.

The infants were very curious about the large paper bag that I brought in and left in the middle of the playroom floor. Simone and Sophia were first to venture over to see what was inside the bag. Molly and Brodey were not far behind. Sophia stuck her head inside the bag and pulled out a blue purse, which she carried over to the climber to investigate. Simone felt that the black backpack went better with her ensemble. She put the straps around her neck, and off she went.

Brodey could not decide what item to choose, and after examining them all thoroughly, he selected a white purse that he then draped over his body. Molly chose a black, shiny purse and a red gift bag. All of the children moved about the room with their new acquisitions, opening and closing them, filling them with blocks and small toys, dumping them out, and repeating the actions. The purses and bags remained in the classroom for two weeks, and the children never grew tired of them. They seemed to find new and different ways of playing with them every day.

Chart 6.1

MATERIALS FOR PRETEND PLAY	
Open-ended Toys & Materials	**Structured Toys & Materials**
• Are flexible • Stimulate imagination • Have universal appeal for children of all ages and all cultures	• Have a distinct purpose • Are used primarily to imitate real-life • Are closely related to culture and age, that is what the child knows and understands
• Building blocks • Dolls • Pieces of cloth & scraps of wood or Styrofoam • Play dough/clay • Found material (e.g., stones, shells, empty cans and containers, boxes of all shapes and sizes, wool & ribbon, fancy paper, chop sticks, food packaging trays)	• Ride-on toys • Stacking & nesting toys • Puzzles and games • Replicas such as Fisher Price farm & train set • Theme related costumes • Doctors bag • Firemen's hats & gear • Aprons, baking equipment • Empty cans and food packages, cash register, toy money

Parents know the frustration of having their four-year-old whine, "I'm bored," when their room is filled to overflowing with toys. There are a number of reasons why children get turned off their toys and want something new. Some of these factors are out of our hands, but others can be controlled by limiting what they receive, rotating some of the toys that don't seem to be used often, and making sure that there is plenty of found material available for them to use in play.

> *For help in selecting toys, check out sites on the Internet. One excellent resource is the Canadian Toy Testing Council, a nonprofit organization working for parents to assess toys. Each year they publish* The Toy Report, *in which they rate hundreds of new toys on the market for design, function, durability, and play value.*

The Big Business of Toys

Many of today's toys are marketed for their economic value rather than their value as play props. This trend began in 1984 when the United States Federal Communications Commission deregulated media-linked toys. Lucrative lines of toys quickly found their way onto the market based on figures from television and movies. Many of these toys were action figures condoning violence and aggressive play. Ninja Turtles, Power Rangers, and a whole gamut of other superheroes that are rated by the television or movie regulations for older children are sold as toys for children as young as four or five years old. This trend shows no sign of slowing down as even dolls have become sex symbols with slinky costumes and beauty pageant looks.

One consideration that will help parents choose wisely is the flexibility of the toy.

- Can the child play with it in a variety of ways?

- Does it challenge the child's ingenuity?

- Is it a toy that will have appeal at any age and stage?

- Can more than one child play with this toy?

For parents whose children have too many toys, it is time to take stock and do some rearranging. Try creating three piles of toy based on the following considerations:

- What toys remain the child's favorites?

- What toys has the child outgrown?

- What toys has the child not played with for a time?

Things to Keep in Mind When Selecting Toys

There are so many toys on the market that a parent can feel overwhelmed trying to make a selection. Sales pitches do little more than add to the confusion. There are tried and true toys that have been enjoyed by babies the world over. These include blocks, rattles, dolls, and stuffed toys. Here are some things to consider when making your choices:

- Does it appeal to the senses? Babies enjoy playing with toys that are brightly colored, make a noise, and have an interesting feel to them.

- Is there too much stimulation? Keep it simple. For example, when faced with a play station with too many attachments, a baby is likely to end up flitting from one thing to another without really exploring any of the objects.

- Could this toy appeal to both boys and girls? While boys and girls do play differently with gender-related toys, they should have a selection that cuts across stereotypical lines. Dolls and homemaking items should be available to boys. Sports equipment and construction toys should be available for girls.

- Is this toy safe? The toy should not have any sharp edges, attached string, or small pieces that can be detached. What is safe for a two-year-old may not be for a three-month-old.

- Is the toy solidly made? Infants and toddlers can be very hard on their toys as they bang them, drop them, and put them through every manner of crash test. Good toys can withstand this normal treatment without coming apart or shattering. Toys that are battery operated need to be carefully checked on a regular basis to make sure that the battery is not leaking acid.

If there are toys that are clearly of no further interest or use, these can be donated to a local charity. Before doing this, however, the child should be given a say. Although a toy may be from an earlier stage, a child may be reluctant to part with it.

Once it has been decided what toys to keep, the next step is to select some toys to keep out and others to put away for a while. Too many toys overwhelm the child and result in loss of interest. On a regular basis, you should rotate the toys so that there is some novelty to the collection.

Organizing and displaying the toys is an important consideration for parents and teachers. The way toys are stored has a bearing on whether they will be used and on how they are used. If everything is thrown into a big basket, a child tends to neglect those on the bottom. Putting labels and perhaps a logo from the box on the front of a shelf helps to focus attention on the toy and remind the child where each toy is stored.

It will be necessary for a parent to help with the tidy up until the child is old enough to handle this task independently. Although time consuming at first, in the long run it will save many hours of aggravation and cleanup as well as developing a habit of responsibility for one's own things.

What Can We Do to Help?

➢ Finding time and space for play is directly connected to our *attitudes* toward play. Create an atmosphere of acceptance for the mess and noise of play. This phase of your child's life is over all too soon. In the early years, your home is your child's world. How sad if at every turn his play is cut short by admonitions to "pick up those toys," "don't make so much noise," or "you know you're not allowed to play there."

➢ Have a family meeting and take stock of how time is being spent. Set up a schedule for the hectic times such as meal preparation when Mom and Dad take turns having playtime with the children. This frees the other parent to prepare the meals and lunches for the next day. When children are old enough, they can help with the meals and then have time for play.

➤ Make use of community resources. Most local libraries and community centers provide programs for young children. These involve everything from organized story time to performances by children's musicians and theater groups. Take time to attend these events with your children. We tend to think that children are exposed to so much on television and film that they don't need these experiences, but there is a world of difference between a television show and seeing a live performance. This is one way to encourage children to move away from a steady diet of television and have the reassurance that the subject matter will be appropriate for young children.

Being an architect of the playscape means providing the toys and materials as well as the experiences and permission to play. The toys and materials we provide do not have to be fancy. Basic toys such as a soft, cuddly bear or a colorful string of play beads are inexpensive. Everyday objects found around the home, such as assorted plastic container lids, can provide countless hours of play and learning. The important thing is to value play and give your child the room and the encouragement that lets him know that play is special in your home or classroom.

In early development, a playful learning environment is everything. Childhood occurs once in a lifetime, and it passes all too quickly. If you do nothing else, make sure your children are free to play. Have faith in their ingenuity to find things to play with. By simply being present as you fold the laundry or make dinner, children will get on with their play.

7

Outdoor Play

It is unfortunate that children can't design their outdoor play environments. Research on children's preferences show that if children had the design skills to do so, their creations would be completely different from the areas called playgrounds that most adults design for them. Outdoor spaces designed by children would not only be fully naturalized with plants, trees, flowers, water, dirt, sand, mud, animals and insects, but also would be rich with a variety of play opportunities of every imaginable type. If children could design their outdoor spaces, they would be rich, developmentally appropriate learning environments where children would want to stay all day.

Randy White and Vicki Stoecklin

The outdoor play environment offers a unique place, full of endless possibilities for play and learning. In an outdoor setting there are no limits on space or exuberance. Equipment is optional and children will work with what is available. The natural world invites play by virtue of its freedom to move and leap and rummage about in exploration.

Physical Development in Outdoor Play

Play helps children practice three kinds of movements: balance, coordination of large muscles, and coordination of small muscles.

On average the third year of life is thought to be the most physically active.

For detailed discussion of the stages in physical development see Motor Development and Movement Experiences. D. L. Gallahue (1976).

Chart 7.1

PHYSICAL DEVELOPMENT IN OUTDOOR PLAY	
Basic Skills	**Play Experiences**
Balance Balance allows children to maintain their equilibrium while moving the body in a wide variety of ways including stretching, twisting, bending, stopping, and landing.	• Balance boards • Climbers • Swings • Stilts • Rocking horse
Coordinating Large Muscles During the period between ages two and six the coordination of the large muscles develops rapidly allowing for such actions as: walking, running, jumping, skipping, and galloping.	• Climbers • Skipping ropes • Hoops • Tunnels • Riding/ pedal toys • Pull toys • Music and movement activities • Jolly jumper • Jungle gym
Coordinating the Fine Muscles There is a huge difference in the way in which a two-year-old handles a crayon and the way in which a five-year-old does the same thing. It is development of the fine muscles that allows a child to throw a ball, and eventually catch one, strike a target as well as gain control over small objects and tools and tasks such as tying shoelaces.	• Balls • Bats and other kinds of rackets • Beanbags • Target games • Building blocks • Interlocking blocks • Craft tools such as scissors, glue stick, paints, and brushes • Stacking and nesting toys

In earlier times, childhood was equated with being active in an outdoor environment, but this is no longer so. Today's child spends a large portion of her time indoors, passively watching television or playing electronic games, often in isolation from other children. In an article "Is the Canadian childhood obesity epidemic related to physical inactivity?" M. S. Tremblay and J. D. Willms (2003) found that TV watching and video games are risk factors for being overweight. These findings are similar to the data from other countries, including the United States. Other studies have not been as conclusive (Vanderwater, Shim, and Caplovitz 2004). What does seem clear from the studies and from observation is that there is a link between inactivity and obesity, and TV and video games, for the most part, are inactive pastimes. The video-game producers are taking this connection seriously. Wii, a new gaming system from Nintendo, is being advertised as combating obesity since it requires the video-game players to actively play the game. This system includes a number of sports games, such as tennis, golf, and wrestling.

According to a study by the National Longitudinal Survey of Children and Youth in Canada, conducted in 1999, 37 percent of children ages two to eleven were identified as overweight and 18 percent as obese. The American Obesity Association found that 30 percent of children ages six to eleven were overweight and 15 percent were obese. For further information see Statistics Canada, Human Resources Development Canada, and United States National Institutes of Health..

At a time when children are getting less and less outdoor exercise, they are being deprived of play on all fronts. In shocking numbers, today's children are at risk of obesity and all of the health problems that stem from being grossly overweight. These include type 2 diabetes, bone loss, asthma, high blood pressure, and depression. These issues add up to a compelling case for quality physical activity, of which outdoor play is the primary means for young children.

This might seem to be an argument in favor of enrolling children in organized sports at an early age, and as a well-intentioned response to the need for physical activity, parents are doing just that. Everything from swimming to soccer is offered for preschoolers. Much has been written about the pros and cons of organized sports versus the traditional unstructured games and activities of play. While there can be benefits to structured classes given by a knowledgeable professional, these are never a replacement for play.

New Uses of Playgrounds

Traditionally, public playgrounds in urban settings such as parks, schoolyards, and apartment complexes focused almost exclusively on physical development. Slides, swings, climbers, and seesaws are important to the gross motor development of the arms and legs. These traditional pieces of equipment are also important for developing balance and control over movement. As important as this function is, this type of equipment tends to be inflexible and have a single purpose. This equipment does little to promote social development, since the child is usually performing the activity alone. Other than size, little or no consideration is given to accommodating the changing developmental needs of children. Over the past three decades, there has been some much-needed research into how children use the playground. This information is changing the look of the outdoor play space.

Playgrounds today are seen as places not only for physical development but for social and imaginative play as well. There is also more attention given to the varying developmental needs of children, from toddlers through the middle years. This has brought changes to the type of equipment provided at the playground. Where once children found mainly large muscle equipment, including swings, slides, and climbers, today additional items are added to encourage pretend play and games. An open playhouse, a climbing dome, and stationary ride-on toys all invite children to pretend. The equipment is sufficiently flexible to allow children of different ages and stages to play together..

Studies have shown that children prefer equipment that can be adapted to their play ideas rather than fixed, single-purpose items traditionally associated with a playground. Action-oriented equipment such as ride-on toys, swinging tires, and climbing domes lend themselves to imaginative, social play. In a study comparing indoor and outdoor play in nursery school, Michael Henniger (1985) found that boys and older children engaged in more pretend play outdoors than in. He suggested that the open space and flexible equipment invited a wider range of themes. Outdoors, noise and mess are not a factor in the exuberant play of boys. Another set of studies, (Frost 1992;

Frost and Sunderlin 1985) found that the younger children preferred equipment that encouraged sociodramatic play, such as a playhouse or construction toys, while the older children played more games with rules. In fact 1 percent of kindergarten children played games with rules, while 18 percent of second graders played games with rules. This is consistent with developmental patterns of play as described in Chapter 3.

Perhaps the biggest change in playgrounds is the focus on connecting with nature. When the traditional playgrounds were first designed, children had more access to nature in their everyday lives. They spent far more time outdoors playing than most children today. There was less concern for safety even in urban settings. Children were free to explore ravines and wood lots. This has all changed with what has been called *bogeyman paranoia*. Not without cause, parents are afraid to let their children out of their sight. At the same time there is a growing appreciation of the unique gifts of nature. We as a civilization are re-awakening to the need to be vigilant stewards of nature's resources.

Designing playgrounds that connect our children with nature is becoming a strong trend. Ecologists and environmentalists stress the importance of reaching children at an early age in order to develop their sense of wonder and responsibility toward the natural world. Providing playgrounds that are open to the changes of climate and season helps children respond to the natural rhythms of life. It makes children aware of the vast variety of life on the planet.

To this end, interesting outdoor play spaces are popping up that accommodate goals that include social development, exploration, and the opportunity to experience the natural world. A playground that addresses these goals is built around the natural features of the landscape. Paved lots with a collection of fixed swings, slides, and climbers are becoming a thing of the past. New parks and playgrounds set in green areas with natural hills, boulders, streams, and flexible equipment are replacing the more sterile environments. Often sand is used under the climber and other large equipment to soften any fall. Natural materials, including water and sand, are accessible.

Outdoors in a well-planned playground there will be spaces that have shrubs, trees, and small gardens that attract insects, birds, butterflies, and small ground animals. There will be a place for a tended garden, perhaps for herbs, vegetables, or flowers. Wildflowers will have space to grow and provide a panorama of color and changing interest over the spring, summer, and fall. These experiences of nature are vitally important to instill awareness and care for the natural world. Children who are bored are not children who investigate the natural world. The infinite variety cannot help but capture interest and imagination.

One of the things parents can do is encourage children from an early age to take an interest in the natural world by showing this passion themselves. Instilling respect and awe for the natural world can be extended beyond the playground as we take children on walks into a wooded area or ravine. This, of course, assumes that we as adults have not lost our connection with the earth and its wonders. Perhaps awakening a sense of wonder in our young children will reawaken it in us.

Four-year-old Liam loves nothing more than puttering in the garden beside his father, who has a landscaping business. Already Liam is intrigued by the many tiny creatures he finds in the garden. He is learning that watching the toad in its natural habitat is a wonderful experience, but he must not pick him up, put him in a jar, or otherwise disrupt his world. He has learned that these tiny creatures will not survive if handled and mistreated.

In addition to commercial designs, many wonderful playgrounds are now available that reflect the broader purposes of outdoor play. One of the most exquisite playgrounds I have visited is Spiral Garden located at the Bloorview Kids Rehab in Toronto. This rehabilitation center serves children with disabilities and has facilities for inpatients, outpatients, and day patients, as well as continuing care. Spiral Garden is based on the belief that interaction with the natural and creative processes promotes healing. Spiral Garden brings children with and without disabilities together under a canopy of trees to play and learn. In this outdoor world children tend an organic garden, sculpt a world out of clay, and work with wood and other natural materials to create their own artistic monuments and celebrate community through storytelling.

So successful is this playground that its staff have become involved in several international initiatives to bring play and healing to traumatized children. Recently the artistic coordinator of Bloorview's Center for the Arts, of which Spiral Garden is a vital component, traveled to Tamil Nadu with the International Institute for Children's Rights and Development to train local staff for outdoor play programs designed to rebuild a sense of trust in the natural world. Staff members from Spiral Garden have also participated in establishing similar programs, notably the Butterfly Peace Garden in Balticaloa, Sri Lanka, and have given workshops in Bogota, Columbia, and the West Bank.

Observing children playing and participating in the many activities of Spiral Garden demonstrates how much pleasure the natural outdoor environment brings to children of all ages, all cultures, and all abilities. Spiral Garden is a testament to the forward thinkers who first imagined such a play space in what, at the time, was simply an unused wood lot backing onto a ravine. Staff artists, visiting artists, and storytellers come to this garden to share their time and talents with the children, and both are the richer for the experience. This is a living monument to play and its power to bring the joy of learning to children.

A project of the scope of Spiral Garden may be well beyond your reach, but it shows that an outdoor playground is more than just a place to keep children busy while they get some fresh air. In conjunction with other parents and community groups, you may be surprised at what can be done.

Backyard Playgrounds

Children are not able to explore the nooks and crannies of their own neighborhoods as did children in earlier generations. For this reason, parents who can do so are anxious to bring the playground experience to their own backyard. While the backyard will have limits due to size of the lot and cost of equipment, there are some distinct advantages of a private space over a public facility.

- Equipment can be selected specifically for the developmental stages of the children, with provision for changes as their needs evolve.

- An enclosed playhouse or a shed can become part of the backyard play space, while for obvious reasons an enclosure is not suitable for a public playground. If you do not have access to a permanent structure, a large empty appliance box will do just fine.

- Equipment can be improvised and homemade. With the number and size of the children using the equipment it does not have to be as sturdy as that in a public place. That does not mean it can be unsafe, but simply does not have to take the wear and tear of a large volume of players.

- All equipment should be checked regularly for safety.

  o Are there any sharp corners or pieces that could harm a child?

  o Is there any way children could catch a scarf or even their hair while moving on the apparatus?

  o Does the sandbox have a protective cover when not in use?

  o Is the equipment, particularly the homemade items, free from toxic materials?

Public playgrounds such as those in a schoolyard or community center must take into account the risk of vandalism and potential safety hazards. For this reason, the large equipment is fixed and highly durable. Whether attached to a community center, a school, or in the backyard, there is some inexpensive equipment that can be made available to the children to extend their play. Such items as a sawhorse, ladder, tires, wire spools, and barrels offer a range of play opportunities. These items can be stored in an outdoor shed or other available storage space when not in use. The advantage of this kind of equipment is that children can use it to extend the existing fixed items, and it can be combined and recombined to extend their play.

In addition to providing the equipment, we must make sure that there is sufficient space for the ride-on toys and the flow of traffic within the playground. If the area is too congested or poorly laid out, unnecessary conflicts will arise and disrupt the play. We must be selective in putting out new equipment, keeping in mind that something new sparks renewed interest in play.

For excellent information on planning an outdoor play space, see *The Great Outdoors: Restoring Children's Right to Play Outside* by Mary S. Rivkin (NAEYC).

This little boy cannot climb without the help of a railing, but that doesn't stop him from finding a way.

Chart 7.2

NON-COMMERCIAL EQUIPMENT FOR OUTDOOR PLAY	
Improvised Equipment	**What you'll need**
Tunnels	• Large round container - garbage can, laundry basket, barrel • Cut out bottom and smooth any rough edges. • Purchase cloth tunnels such as those used for dog agility training. Select the length according to size and age of children
Balance Beams	• Horizontal wooden logs • Lengths of 2x4 planks • Posts of varying heights dug into the ground to make a pathway
Climbers	• Large tires fastened together and hung against a wall • Large piece of drift wood or tree branch placed on the ground • Ladder placed along the ground (older children can use it to climb up) • Kitchen stair steps
Structures	• Saw horses and planks • Blankets, sleeping bag, tent • Appliance boxes with one side open for entrance

Upper body development	• Make punching bag by stuffing a duffle bag or shoe bag and hanging it from a tree.
	• An improvised sand pit for digging
	  o Place a large truck tire on a platform of bricks
	  o Fill the inside with sand
	  o The bricks will provide drainage
	  o Cover when not in use.
	• In backyard playground designate a patch of garden in which the child is free to dig and make mud pies

What Can We Do To Help?

➢ Playgrounds don't charge membership fees. They are there to provide children with unlimited opportunities for physical development and socialization. The equipment, particularly in newer facilities, offers a wide range of activity for developing the large muscles while at the same time providing for social development through play. Don't just sit there. Get involved. You can combine your own needs for physical activity with that of your children.

➤ Most urban communities now have lovely parks and playgrounds as a standard feature. When you are feeling stressed and overwhelmed, take this opportunity to relax and restore your own energies in the peaceful setting of a park. If you are fortunate enough to live in a rural setting, the possibilities for outdoor play are limitless. You may not have the expensive equipment of a large, urban playground, but climbing trees, walking along fences, and swinging from branches were the first outdoor playgrounds.

➤ If your community playground or school playground is not up to par, get involved with other parents in fixing it up. Organize a community play day for children and parents. You might invite a local early childhood teacher to show parents how to play with their children and to explain the learning that is taking place. As suggested in the section on toys, good quality blocks, ride-on toys, and other larger equipment can be expensive, but you can often find these at reduced prices at garage sales, flea markets, and second-hand shops. With a little cleaning and perhaps paint, these reclaimed items may be as good as new. Many years ago, a group of junior kindergarten teachers picked up a dozen ride-on toys and wagons at a flea market. They spent a Saturday with screwdrivers, and with some help from husbands and paint cans, they equipped their classrooms with an amazing collection of these expensive toys for next to nothing.

While your children are young is the time to recapture your own sense of wonder. This will set your children on a path toward environmental responsibility far more surely than all the lectures could ever do. Respect for the environment begins in our own backyard. Young children are naturally attracted to creatures that creep and fish that swim. Show them how to watch and take delight from these small creatures.

If we want to address serious health issues such as childhood obesity or addiction to computer games and media superheroes, we need to provide our children with the means to explore the outdoors. They need to be able to climb and swing and pretend in a safe outdoor play space. We need to take our children to natural settings where they can observe and investigate the world of nature. These resources are never that far away and don't charge admission. This is one of the lifelong interests you can give your child.

To keep alive his inborn sense of wonder a child needs the companionship of at least one adult who can share it, rediscovering with him the joy, excitement and mystery of the world we live in.

Rachel Carson

8

The Adult in a Supporting Role

> Research has revealed that, far from being harmful or disruptive, adult involvement often enriches the quality of children's play and is beneficial in other ways as well. The value of adult participation in play has been demonstrated in play training experiments and observational studies of play in the home and in the preschool classroom.
>
> James Johnson, James Christie, and Thomas Yawkey

Adults instinctively recognize play as a way of connecting with a newborn baby. They see the baby's delight when they play games such as tickling, rocking horse, bouncing and swinging, singing and dancing with them. Joining children in play does not have to be reserved for newborns but provides an excellent means of establishing a positive relationship between a child and adults. Recapturing our lost sense of playfulness is a gift our children give to us.

Supporting Learning through Play: A Matter of Attitude

Perhaps the most valuable way we can help our children learn through play is by honoring their right to play. Our attitude toward play will determine to a large extent how much our children learn through play. If we believe that play is an essential means of healthy growth and development, we will find time and space as well as provide the necessary materials. If on the other hand, we sign them up for lessons in everything from violin to gymnastics, with no time left for spontaneous learning through play, children will get the message.

Our attitude comes through in how we react when our children are playing. The time when play, and in particular sociodramatic play, is at its richest is the time when there will be the most mess and noise. Children spontaneously change roles and actions, discarding one prop in favor of another, taking off one costume and adding another. If they are excited, which they are likely to become, the voices rise and the noise level escalates. These are characteristics of creativity not negative behavior. The dolly is thrown down on the floor as the child changes from playing mother to going shopping.

Once we recognize the significance of play, we can more easily accept the noise and the mess of play and join in the fun. When speaking with teachers about play, I would often ask them to train their eyes and their ears to distinguish between the noise and mess of chaos and the noise and mess of creativity. There is a distinct quality that can help parents as well as teachers make decisions about when to intervene and when to let the learning soar through creative play. The noise and mess of discord is quite distinct from the joyful noise of play.

A second way that we as adults support learning through play is by providing experiences that enrich the child's mind. Pretend play becomes increasingly complex as children gain wider and wider access to the world outside their home. By giving your children experiences with people and places in your community, they will have a larger range of roles and topics to explore in their pretend play. They come to know what people do when they go shopping, ride public transit, go to a garden center, or whatever is commonplace in your community.

With a little effort you may find other interesting people and places to visit right on your own doorstep. I am always surprised that we often ignore what is right in front of us. As a classroom teacher, one of the first things I did when I went to a new school was to check out the community. One year, when assigned a second-grade class, I found a beekeeper quite close to our community. He was pleased to bring a hive and other paraphernalia to our class as a resource for a study of honeybees. That same year, when our hamster hurt his foot, I contacted a veterinarian who was within walking distance of the school, and one snowy morning off we went, all forty second graders with our hamster cozily tucked into a woolen mitt. What a great opportunity this was to learn about care for animals.

Another way in which we feed children's imagination is through literature. Stories, whether read or told, introduce readers to places and people far beyond their own circle. Stories can spark humor or fear or excitement. You will see in sociodramatic play and in their first attempts at story writing the structure of events and the different ways characters can be portrayed. Children who have heard the classic folk and fairy tales love to recreate these stories in their play.

One morning, as Gregory and several others are playing in the home center, he announces: "Come on, guys. We're going to play Cinderella." The others move right into the theme as he assigns the roles.

"You be the fairy godmother," he says to Samantha. "You have the pretty dress."

He says to Dora, with whom he is often in conflict, "You be the ugly sister."

Gregory assigns the part of Cinderella to Zoe.

He is the stepmother, and as he puts on an apron, he exclaims, "We're going to have a party tonight and Cinderella can't come! Have to get ready!"

He then orders the stepsisters to get busy sweeping the floor, cleaning the windows, and so on.

Gregory is an advanced player and is able to sustain the episode through a number of digressions. Brandon, a less mature boy, enters the home center and announces, "I'll be the Daddy."

Gregory in exasperation says," There are no daddies in Cinderella. You can be the prince or the mouse."

Dora plunks down on a chair and says, "I can't go to the dance 'cause I don't have no date."

Once again Gregory must resolve the problem, this time by using his authority as the stepmother.

"Ugly stepsisters don't have dates!" he says.

They argue back and forth until he drops out of role and tells her if she doesn't play right, she can't stay.

This episode never results in a "play" about Cinderella but a reenactment based on the events of the story. It shows the difficulty of sustaining an episode of sociodramatic play based on a story that is not familiar to all of the participants.

A third way that adults support play is as an initiator. One way of getting the ball rolling is by making a playful suggestion. Another is what I call capturing the moment. Capturing the moment occurs when children are already caught up in their play and we introduce a suggestion or a prop that moves the play to a different level.

No matter how we are involved in play, we need to recognize the developmental characteristics at each stage and hold realistic expectations for how our children will play. We must also resist the tendency to "play teacher." By that I mean imposing direction in the middle of play in order to teach.

I was sitting in a doctor's waiting room one morning when I noticed three little children playing with a shape-sorting toy. The two boys were around ages three and four. The little girl, who was approaching two years of age, stood off to the side watching. The boys were very accurate in how they placed the shape pieces. When their mother came out of the examining room, the boys left and the little girl sat down with the toy. She began to randomly place the pieces. The little girl's mother, who was watching, sat down beside her and began to show her how to play "properly." The little girl promptly moved away and selected something else to play with.

What was going on? Should the mother not have joined in? Why did the little girl leave? This is a clear example of having inappropriate developmental expectations. At this stage, this two-year-old simply needs to explore the pieces and experiment with them. She is not interested in solving the puzzle. The mother on the other hand wants her "to play it right." It is very important to adapt expectations to developmental levels. Perhaps this was not the appropriate time to interfere. Perhaps the mother could have watched and learned something about her daughter's thinking. Does she recognize that the shapes are different? Can she recognize that some shapes are the same but different in size? These understandings will come as she experiments.

Chart 8.1

PRACTICAL SUGGESTIONS FOR SUPPORTING PLAY	
The Role of the Adult	**Things to Remember**
Provide the playscape. • make toys and materials available • have a place to play	• If you provide the basic materials as well as a place to play, children are likely to be quite independent in their play.
Feed the imagination. • give children a wide range of experiences • read stories • where possible, attend live performances suitable for children	• Explore places and events close to home. • It's never too early to begin to build a collection of books for your child • Local libraries and community festivals are good places to find live entertainment and events designed for children.
Get the ball rolling. • respect age and developmental level • set rules to ensure safety of the children • expect children to respect the toys and play property • make suggestions that tie in with their own world	• Don't disrupt the play unnecessarily • It doesn't matter so much what the children play as the fact that they are playing.

Supporting Learning as a Play Partner

Being an effective play partner means that we join in the play, not to direct it toward some goal we might have, but to stimulate the play. Our participation can encourage language development and thinking as we talk to our children, ask them questions, and take on the dialogue of our character.

Being a play partner means that we respect the children's ideas and don't try to impose our own hidden agenda on them. They are very quick to pick up on insincerity. They intuitively know the difference between someone who genuinely is interested in their play and those who are merely making a show of it. It has been said that children instinctively know who will play with them.

Spontaneous pretend play is thought to be the most important form of play in terms of development and learning. Many studies have shown that the participation of an adult in pretend play improves the experience for children. The benefits of adult participation in pretend play, however, depend on how well we understand our role as a play partner.

One of the first things to keep in mind is that we should *enter by invitation*. By age three, as children increasingly engage in pretend play, they become independent and may not want an adult to intrude in their make-believe. If we try to force ourselves on them, they are likely to leave and turn to some other activity. On the other hand, if we see that the pretend play is getting very repetitive and lacking in imagination, we can spark it up by bringing something new to the situation or creating a crisis.

We need to remember that *play belongs to the children*. When you have the privilege of being invited into the child's pretend play, it must be on his terms. You will be assigned a role, one of lesser importance, and the child will treat you accordingly. You will be bossed around and told what to do and expected to stay in role and act accordingly.

The kindergarten children and I were playing reindeers. As we rode in the pretend sleigh, one of the reindeer noticed that the children in the home center were playing restaurant.

"I'm hungry," she said. "Let's get something to eat."

We traipsed into the restaurant, sat down at the table, and one of the girls came to take our order.

"What do you want for lunch?" she asked.

"Roast reindeer," I said.

The other reindeer did not think this funny, and the boss reindeer, dropping out of character, said to me, "If you don't play right, you can't play."

After apologizing, I was reinstated.

Our participation should *be authentic*. Once we are in role, we follow the children's lead. When the reindeer get into the sleigh and Rudolf turns the key with a "brummmm, brummmm," we don't correct the logic. Children take their pretend play very seriously and expect you to do the same. They do not want you to be silly. They want you to pretend.

Andy is playing by himself in the home center of his junior kindergarten classroom. As his teacher, Mrs. McCarthy, goes by he says, "Want to come for lunch?"

"That would be nice," says Mrs. McCarthy. "What are we having?"

"Soup," answers Andy.

By now Erica has come along and is watching, obviously wanting to join in. Andy ignores her.

"Don't you think we should invite Erica?" asks Mrs. McCarthy.

It is obvious that Andy does not think much of this suggestion. Reluctantly, to please his teacher, he does ask Erica to join them but refuses to give her a chair.

"They're all taken!" he says, although three are empty. Mrs. McCarthy moves over and gives her chair to Erica.

Andy then proceeds to plunk some bowls and pans and cutlery on the table in no particular order. Mrs. McCarthy distributes them but says nothing.

"What do you want to drink?" he asks. "Chocolate milk or juice?"

"Do you have any tea?"

"Sure." He pretends to pour tea into a cup and hands it to her.

"What about Erica?" asks Mrs. McCarthy.

With a big sigh Andy says, "Erica, what do you want?"

"Tea," she answers.

As they pick up their cups to drink the tea, Mrs. McCarthy comments, "Careful, it's hot," and sips away.

This is a fine illustration of authenticity. Mrs. McCarthy did not talk down to the children, nor did she act silly. It was as though they were engaged in a real tea party. By suggesting that they invite Erica to join them, she opened the door for Andy to add another play partner. Although reluctant, he did so to please Mrs. McCarthy. While she encouraged Andy to accept an onlooker, she did not insist or make an issue out of sharing. Once again, she made a suggestion that opened a door without disrupting the flow of the episode.

As play partners we need to *be unobtrusive in our suggestions*. While we need to be unobtrusive, this does not mean that there is no place for our input. It simply means that when we do offer suggestions that could extend the play, we do so in role.

Three-year-old Brianna picks up the toy telephone and pretends to talk to an imaginary friend. Her mother takes up a wooden spoon and has a conversation with Brianna.

"Come for coffee and a donut," Brianna says.

"Why don't we meet at the Tim Horton's?" replies her mother.

"Okay," replies Brianna.

She puts down the telephone, puts her dolly in the stroller, picks up her purse, and pretends to go to the restaurant.

By moving the episode from the setting of a family kitchen to a coffee shop, the mother was encouraging her daughter to use different rituals and roles. The language used would also be more complex. As it turned out, Brianna got distracted and began to change her baby. With no opening for the mother to participate, she remained with Brianna but had little part to play. It is often enough to simply be in attendance.

I've often seen teachers who are uncomfortable with a theme try to redirect the sociodramatic play. This happens particularly when the theme is one of superheroes. There is nothing wrong with introducing an alternative theme, but it should be done as part of the play itself.

Three little boys are replaying an episode from a television action program involving a car crash. They repeat the same sequence of actions a number of times, each time getting more boisterous. Finally, the teacher puts on a white coat that was in the home center, pulls a wagon over to the crash scene, and says, "I'm the emergency guy. What hospital do you want me to take him to?" Without dropping out of character, the two boys pick up the victim, drop him in the wagon, and off they run to the home center that immediately becomes a hospital. Children playing there join in giving treatment, taking his pulse, and even giving him a pretend needle.

This is a clear example of positive intervention. The teacher in role made a suggestion that would extend the play, but the children were free to take up this suggestion or ignore it. She didn't disrupt the flow of their play but made a suggestion that sparked immediate interest. With practice we can become quite skillful at extending play.

Babies thrive on the loving play of a grandparent.

Some parents and teachers are more comfortable as a partner in playing games. They find it easier to play ball or roughhouse than to make-believe. Here again, we need to take care that we respect the child's developmental level as well as the nature of play. We need to remember, for example, that below the age of seven, most children make up rules as they go along. Our participation is about making connections with our children, encouraging them to play, and sometimes serving as a bridge between the less able player and the more advanced ones.

Chart 8.2

BEING A PLAY PARTNER	
When you initiate play either choose a theme or activity that is a favorite or introduce something they haven't seen before.	Try: Bring a new board game, a new puzzle or a toy. Let the children have time to explore it before starting to play. Add some new costumes such as high-heeled shoes, hats or even a play tiara, anything to spark imagination.
If children are already absorbed in their play enter only by invitation. If you are a regular player you will have no difficulty getting in but if you rarely get into a role, they will likely ignore you.	Try: Make a part for yourself that fits in with the theme they are playing. For example: the children are building a space ship. You come over with a helmet or some other prop and tell them you are the count down guy and all is ready for lift off. They better get their seat belts fastened.
Pretend play is a serious business to children and you need to keep your participation authentic. If you are not genuinely interested and involved they will sense this and move on to something else. Don't be looking around watching what else is happening. If you have the privilege of being asked to play, take full advantage both for your own sake and that of the children.	Try: Put on a costume and choose a prop to help you create the role. Listen to the children. Focus on what they are saying and doing. Don't be afraid to add some humor.

118

The playful behavior needed to be an effective play partner does not come naturally to some adults. Perhaps it is the fear of appearing silly, or perhaps their own play was so limited that they did not learn these skills as a child. Whatever the reason, a parent's inability to play can have a negative influence on how well a child thrives through play. I recall being at the Toronto Science Centre one afternoon with a group of teacher candidates. A four-year-old child was visiting the center with his grandmother. He was doing experiments at a sand and water exhibit, and I began to play with him. After about ten minutes, I became aware that a group of my students was gathered, watching what I was doing. "Can you teach us how to do that?" asked one student.

I've thought a good deal about this request, and I'm not sure that I can teach someone with no humor or playfulness to become a play partner, certainly not in the style that I use. Playfulness needs to be genuine. It requires the ability to laugh at one's self. Having said this, however, I firmly believe that everyone can be a play partner to some extent. It will take time to lose the inhibitions that make us too self-conscious to get lost in play.

For those who are afraid of playing, I would offer these suggestions:

- Begin by singing and dancing. Any type of music will do so long as it frees you to move with ease and delight.

- Get involved in playing games and playing with tabletop toys, such as puzzles and board games.

- Read humorous picture books to your child and giggle alongside him as you enjoy the antics of the characters. Ask your children's librarian to help you select appropriate books.

- Put on a simple costume like a cape or a crown. Those who are shy of "performing" may find that it is easier once they change into a character.

Do what's comfortable for you, and gradually you will relax and enjoy play with your child.

What about the Child Who Doesn't Play?

Both at home and at school a child who doesn't play is a concern to parents and teachers. Some children may play fine when alone but can't play well with others. In the early years, failure to join in play is likely related to the child's age, lack of experience with other children, or lower ability with language than those who are playing. It could also be a matter of personality or parental attitudes. Parents who believe that play is a waste of learning time will perhaps unknowingly inhibit the development of their child's play.

Moving from simple, personal pretend play to complex, collaborative sociodramatic play may not be easy for some children. In order to help children who don't or won't play, we need to find out why. In determining whether your child's inability to play well with others is simply a matter of development or perhaps experience with others of his own age, you need to consider the information found in the previous chapter on the social patterns in play. Perhaps your child is not ready to share and cooperate, but given time, development, and experience, he will gain the necessary skills to fully participate in play.

Social experiences go hand in hand with development as the means of learning how to play with others. Children who have had the chance to play with others either outside their own home or with family members naturally learn the skills that are needed for play. The give and take as well as the sharing of toys and space needed for collaborative play grow over time out of social situations. Children who lead isolated lives in the early years don't have this advantage, and as they get older, it becomes increasingly difficult for them to learn these valuable skills.

In conjunction with the social experiences, children learn the language necessary for collaborative play. By age five children who have played with others and enjoyed a solid foundation of socialization are likely to have all of the language they need to participate in play. Sociodramatic play, in particular, places high demands on a child's language skills as the children plan, negotiate, talk in role, and resolve disagreements. Children who haven't been encouraged to get into pretend play will find it difficult to get involved until they learn these language and social skills. They are likely to be onlookers, watching but unable to find a way into the play. They may barge in and do inappropriate things. This gets them quickly ejected from the episode of play.

Another factor that may influence a child's ability to play is personality. The shy, quiet child may prefer quietly playing with the blocks or reading a picture book. If the child is content to play alone, then we respect that and take advantage of other experiences, such as singing games, to get him involved. Over time as he makes friends, the pretend play should become collaborative, but it won't happen until he is comfortable.

In the early years, parental attitudes may be at the root of reluctance to play. If a child has been discouraged from playing, especially from pretend play, he will enter school with negative feelings toward play. A parent might unwittingly send this message by drumming home the need to keep clean and tidy. Parents of these children sometimes complain that their child is bored, and in the absence of play, he likely is. Play offers such rich learning that given the opportunity, every child should find satisfaction and challenge in participating in play.

None of these factors is a serious problem. For the most part, given time and experience children will grow out of their reluctance or inability to join in play. If the problem seems to be either developmental or simply a lack of experience in playing with other children, encourage the others to include him. Have a more mature player take him as a play partner. At first he will be given the role of the baby or the dog, but at least he is in with the others. As he gains language and social skill, he will become an equal player.

It may be difficult for other young children to make the necessary adjustments for this child. In that case, you will need to serve as a bridge between this child and the other players. It isn't enough to place this child among the others and tell them to play together. You need to create a role for him and help him get into role without being disruptive.

Ethan was an only child from a very protective home. He did not attend daycare or junior kindergarten and rarely got to play with others. When he came to senior kindergarten, he tended to play by himself. At first this was fine with him, but as the months unfolded, he was seen more and more often on the sidelines watching the sociodramatic play. His senior kindergarten teacher suggested to the others that they invite him to join in. This was not very satisfactory, since he generally didn't do what was expected. One morning, the children were playing at having a party. They asked Ms. Gates if she wanted to come to their party. "Great," she said. "Can I bring my new boyfriend?" With that she took Ethan by the hand and led him in. She found a chair for him, and they joined the pretend party. Ms. Gates chatted with him as well as the others. After bringing Ethan with her several times, he was soon joining in on his own.

A more serious cause for concern is that of the withdrawn child. This child may well be experiencing depression and feelings of rejection. We don't like to think of depression in connection with children, but it can be very real. There are clear differences between the quiet child and the withdrawn one. A quiet child will be seen taking everything in. During story time or activities that are favorites, this child will obviously enjoy participating. The withdrawn child, on the other hand, seems uncomfortable in all situations. This child does not want attention and may go unnoticed. A child who is a loner at this early age is missing out on valuable social development and is likely to pay the price in later life. A series of studies (Rubin and Coplan 1998) found that preschool children who were nonsocial or withdrawn were more likely than those who play well with others to experience peer rejection, social anxiety, loneliness, depression, and negative self-esteem in later childhood and adolescence. The nonsocial and withdrawn behaviors also seem to have negative consequences on academic success. This is indeed cause for concern.

Another cause for concern is the bully. This is the child who uses physical force to intimidate his peers. He is likely to be disruptive. While other children of his age are beginning to build a foundation for empathy, he remains self-absorbed and indifferent to the needs and feelings of others. This child is at risk of becoming a violent teenager and developing long-term antisocial behavior. These children may play, but they will tend toward dark themes and hurtful actions.

In both cases, that is, the withdrawn child and the bully, it is essential that the teacher work closely with the family and other caregivers to get to the bottom of the problem. This is a time when a family may need outside professional assistance. This can usually be arranged through a family doctor or the public health system. The important thing is to get help early. These serious problems that manifest themselves in the inability to play won't go away with time.

While specialized help is important, there are things we can do to address the concerns with both the withdrawn child and the bully. For the withdrawn child gently try to engage him as your play partner, perhaps in a board game or in putting together a table toy. Take notice of him by making eye contact, smiling, and praising him when he ventures out of his shell. Give him small errands to do and encourage his confidence. Pick up on what he is good at and use this as a basis for drawing him out.

Helping the bully gain self-control and social skill can be a challenge, but it can be done. This is a child who needs very specific limits and logical consequences to his actions. In play this means that you may have to exclude some toys or some activities.

What Can We Do to Help?

> ➢ Play and be playful with your children. Laughter and glee are great antidotes for the stress of everyday life. Whether roughhousing, having a pretend tea party, or making a castle from blocks, these moments spent together in play will last forever.

> ➢ Whether you are influencing play from outside or as an active player, let the children control and lead the play. When invited to be a play partner, take play seriously and participate wholeheartedly. You will be assigned a lesser role and expected to follow along. With experience you will find that you are able to influence what is going on in an unobtrusive way while in role. If this is a new way of playing with your children, give yourself time. It is better to back off than to interfere and cut the play short.

> ➢ Provide experiences that can serve as grist for the imagination mill by taking your children to visit a relative or to play in the park. Take time to stop and watch the goings on at a construction site. Although these experiences may seem unimportant to an adult, they are the stuff of pretend play and learning.

Intervention can play a positive role in strengthening development through play. Positive intervention is based on understanding the nature of play, that is, that it is free, spontaneous, and driven by the child's inner needs. Intervention takes the form of providing the toys, materials, and opportunities to play, as well as serving as a play partner on the child's terms and enriching the child's experiences. There is a vast difference between this type of intervention and what should more properly be called intrusion. Intrusion is when we impose our agenda on the child's play. We direct the play, and our involvement tends to be that of a warden, making sure the children behave as we think they ought. Intrusion sabotages the play process, and therefore, the benefits to development and learning.

The learning that comes about as a result of play does so largely because it is self-directed. Whether it is the themes children choose, the language used, or the way in which they deal with conflict, unless we let children go through the learning process on their own terms, many valuable opportunities are lost.

9

Discipline through Play

Switching gears after work is one of the hardest parts of parenting for many of us who work outside the home. Most jobs fall a bit short in the giggling department. The same can be said for switching gears after the chores part of child-care or homemaking. It is hard to create a giggly space for playtime. The most common ways that adults unwind—TV, alcohol, and naps—are not part of the Playful Parenting agenda and don't take into account the child's needs. Of course parents have needs too, but if the children are merely an aggravation after work, then something needs to change. Setting aside time for high-energy fun, complete with giggles, can be a new way to meet everyone's needs. The hardworking mom or dad gets to unwind, the child gets exuberant playtime, and everyone gets to reconnect.

Lawrence Cohen

No one wants to raise a brat. A parent's worst nightmare is that he might be held hostage by an out-of-control child. This leads to the fear that if they encourage their children to play, parents will lose control over them. Whether it is a scene in the supermarket, a tantrum at bedtime in front of company, or a screaming match in the playground, the prospect of having a child you cannot control causes many parents to adopt a boot camp mentality. The "do as you're told because I say so" approach may work in the short term, but once the child is free from intimidation, she is likely to do the opposite of what she is told. The other problem with this approach is that when control is no longer there, the child has nothing to fall back on. She has not learned to make decisions and live with the consequences. She has not developed self-discipline. In a boot camp style of discipline, the individual does not have choices and therefore never learns to accept the consequences of her actions.

Self-discipline is necessary in order to become a responsible, contributing member of society. Self-discipline is the basis for autonomy, that is, the ability to make thoughtful choices and accept the consequences of one's actions. This becomes a very important quality as children reach their teenage years, when peer pressure exerts such a powerful influence on young people. Autonomy and self-control can provide a child with the means of resisting the appeal of becoming a gang member or wearing grungy clothing because of taunting. Children who have developed autonomy stand on their own two feet and make decisions based on what is right, rather than what someone will think. The roots of autonomous behavior are found in the disciplinary practices of early childhood.

Discipline in the Early Years

Discipline is a way of keeping order that respects the needs and rights of all members of the community. Discipline can be achieved either through punishment or the development of self-control. Punishment leads to negative feelings about self and others. It may alter behavior at the time but does little to help the child change his behavior over the long run. The object of discipline with children is to develop in them the self-discipline needed as adults to behave in a responsible way. Effective discipline practices lead to the development of self-control. In the early years, this is an important aspect of learning because children are beginning to move away from the self-centered perspective to understanding the needs of others. Up until around age five, children don't consider the feelings of others. As they become involved in a wider social circle, this begins to change and with it comes the need for self-control and self-discipline.

Self-discipline does not appear overnight. It takes a long time and many experiences in living with the consequences of one's actions to become established as a way of acting. In the home, self-discipline begins with having your child take responsibility for basic personal needs. Sometimes we resort to rewards as a means of getting children to do what they are told. A child is given money for putting on her own stockings and shoes. She is offered candy in the supermarket if she stops whining. This response reinforces the negative behavior and doesn't teacher children about self-control. It leads to a child who must have everything now or one who will not take no for an answer.

For discipline to lead to self-control the consequences must have a logical connection to the behavior. Understanding the logical consequences of behavior comes as a result of having these consequences directly related to what she has done.

One day as I was getting out of my car at the supermarket, I noticed a young mother struggling with her two-year-old. She wanted to put the little boy into the shopping cart for safety's sake as they crossed the busy parking lot. He was hooting and hollering in protest. She remained very calm and was not embarrassed as several of us looked on. After a minute or two she said, "Unless you stop crying, I won't be able to do the shopping. We'll have to go home." The little boy stopped his tantrum and let her lift him into the cart. As we walked toward the door, I congratulated her on her parenting skills. She was taken aback and obviously pleased to get some validation. "He knows that I would have taken him home," she said. "I've done it before. It's a pain to have to do that, but I figure it's worth it." Several times as I shopped, I saw the two of them happily chatting.

In this anecdote the little boy's mom made him responsible for his actions. She neither gave in to his tantrum nor forced him to behave as she wanted. Rather she gave him a choice—either he could do what he was asked or there would be no shopping. It is obvious that this child was used to this style of discipline. He needed to control his urge to go scampering off through the traffic or suffer the consequences. He was learning that he could not manipulate her through a tantrum. Although it would have been inconvenient for the mom to return home without her groceries, she recognized that in the long run, it was a necessary sacrifice in order to teach her son an important lesson in self-discipline.

One risk in trying to make children responsible for their actions is that we give them too much freedom. Too many choices result in confusion. Too much negotiation before they are ready can only make children feel unprotected. Giving children too much freedom comes from the mistaken notion that if a parent says no, the child will not feel loved or will not see her parent as a friend. Recognizing the importance of maintaining a warm relationship with their children, parents may easily become a friend at the expense of being a parent. Too much freedom to choose can be as destructive as too little. Parents who struggle to find a balance between being too permissive or too rigid should consult with their family doctor, teacher, or even librarian to find sources of help.

Chart 9.1

TWO APPROACHES TO DISCIPLINE	
Authoritarian Discipline	**Playful Discipline**
Authority imposes rules	Self-discipline
Short term results Applies only to this situation	Learning for life Transfers to other similar situations
Leads to compliance Let someone else think for him and makes decisions based on what he is told	Leads to autonomy Think for oneself and make own decisions based on what is right
Punishment doesn't fit with what the child did	Consequence of actions are directly relate to behavior

Cautionary Note:
Too many choices and too much freedom can be as unhealthy as not enough. Permissiveness, that is letting the child have her own way all the time, won't develop self-discipline any more than being overly strict will. During the preschool years, we provide children with choices but do so with consideration for their age. Too many choices and too little guidance will not result in a foundation for autonomy.

Playful Discipline

Playful discipline is a way of interacting with children that doesn't set up a power struggle. Through playful interaction, the relationship between a child and her parent is preserved, while at the same time, she is learning about self-control and behaving responsibly. She is able to understand that what she is doing is not acceptable, but she is loved no less for her misbehavior.

Walking through a supermarket recently, I noticed a young father accompanied by his five-month-old boy sitting in the shopping cart and a three-year-old girl holding his hand. I noticed that he was playing a game with the little girl, making up words as she went along to accompany the correct name. "What are these?" she asked when they stopped in front of the fresh peas. "These are snow peas," he said, "and these are snap peas. Snap! Snap! Snap!" he sang, snapping his fingers against her side with each snap. She began to giggle and imitate the routine with her baby brother, who then also began to giggle. I commented to the little girl about how lucky her baby brother was to have a great sister to play with him. "They do have fun," said the father. "I love bringing them shopping." What a contrast to the all-too-familiar sight of a parent dragging a child kicking and screaming around the store, with the child demanding this and that of the harried parent, causing an embarrassing commotion.

Playful discipline removes the tension that comes when a child doesn't do as the parent expects. When a situation deteriorates into a prolonged power struggle, the adult has to be the one to diffuse the tension, and there is no better way than through playfulness. Whether it is a major disagreement over what to watch on TV or simply a skirmish over eating all of the vegetables on the plate, the use of humor and play is invaluable. It releases the strain on both child and parent.

If playfulness is the natural way a parent interacts with her children, this attitude will carry over into matters of discipline. Parents for whom being playful is not a spontaneous way of interacting can begin with the everyday skirmishes that occur when raising children. Going to bed, eating everything on your plate, and so on can be turned into playful occasions that get the desired results but don't leave the parent and child angry with one another.

Two-year-old Nelly is refusing to go to bed. Her mom has told her twice that it is time. She takes Nelly by the hand, leads her into the bedroom, and tucks her in. She no sooner gets out the door than Nelly comes flying out. "I can't go to bed because there's tigers under there."

"Ahh, those tigers are back," says her mom. "Whatever will we do?"

"We'll give them milk and cookies and they'll go to sleep," says Nelly. The cookies and milk are placed under the bed, and Nelly and her mom crawl into bed.

Before long, Mom says, "Shh! I think they're asleep." She tiptoes out of the room, and no more is heard of Nelly until morning.

Entering into children's pretend play does not diminish a parent's authority. It serves to bridge a child's emerging desire for independence with a parent's need to keep her child safe and healthy. By being playful, a parent can often model desired behavior without having to lecture the child.

Teachers too may find that with so many demands, they resort to authoritarian rule rather than being playful. The problem, however, is that the more we force children into a power struggle, the more time consuming and stressful the situation becomes. Teachers would find their work more joyful if they used playful methods of discipline.

Many years ago as a second-grade teacher, I was assigned a rambunctious group of children. Many struggles occurred as I tried to get them to settle down to the business of school. One day I took the children to a pet shop, where we purchased a hamster. That afternoon, the noise level was deafening, and although they were not doing anything particularly out of line, the looks from other teachers sent a clear message that I did not have control of them. That evening I wrote a letter to the children from Theodore, the hamster, telling them what he thought of the noisy classroom. He told them that he was a nocturnal animal, which meant that he needed to sleep during the day. With all the noise he couldn't get any rest and may have to return to the pet store for some peace and quiet.

I folded the letter and placed it by the cage door. The children were so taken with this that we had a discussion on what we would have to do to make him stay. This began a yearlong communication between the hamster and the children. They took turns writing back. As time went on, a cast of imaginary characters, including Molly Mouse and the Fur Trapper, became regular features of the stories. This became a wonderful means of dealing with issues of discipline and general behavior.

What was important in the hamster letters was that the children themselves were able to set out rules for behavior in the classroom. They knew that if they didn't keep these rules, the hamster would be taken away.

I had not taught many years when I understood the diminishing returns of authoritarian discipline. When the children were unsettled and grumbly with one another, as they were from time to time, instead of scolding them or depriving them of something they enjoyed, I stopped whatever they were doing, gathered them around me and either sang or read a story to them. When things had calmed down, the regular schedule would resume. With seven-year-olds, I was able to then have a discussion about what had gone on and why it wasn't acceptable. The success of these talks was due largely to the playful atmosphere in the room. When it was necessary to address behavioral issues, the children knew that it was the behavior that was in question, not themselves.

Chart 9.2

ADVANTAGES OF PLAYFUL DISCIPLINE
• Child is clear that punishment doesn't diminish relationship between herself and her parent/teacher.
• Power struggles are reduced with both sides left feeling good about themselves.
• Tension is defused and both child and parent are left relaxed.
• Through playful intervention we can model acceptable behavior.
• Child learns a lesson but is not left beaten down by the experience.

How Play Develops Self-Discipline and Social Skills

Play is one of the most powerful means a child has to develop self-control. Contrary to our assumptions that play is a free-for-all, there are strictly kept rules that children intuitively understand. Such things as staying in role, doing theme-appropriate actions, and accepting direction from the lead player are but a few of these implicit rules. Keeping these rules requires a high level of self-discipline, and from an early age, children themselves will regulate the behavior of the other players.

Experiencing the logical consequences of behavior occurs naturally in play. If a child tries to disrupt play, then the other players will reject her. If she is always taking the best props and costumes, others won't play with her. If a child is a showoff at the expense of the other children, they will leave her behind and move to another activity. Whatever the nature of the self-centered behavior, the consequences are the same. The child does not get to play with the others. In time she comes to see that what she does affects what happens to her.

Taking one's place within a play community requires self-discipline. Turn-taking, sharing, cooperating, communicating, and collaborating are all required during play. These skills are at the heart of self-discipline. Children who must always have their own way or cannot wait while others have a turn will not be accepted into the social world of their peers. We should remember, however, that children under the age of seven put their own needs first. Play presents a long pathway toward true collaboration, with many stumbling blocks and lapses on the way.

Problems that need disciplinary action are often those related to strong feelings and strong emotions. Play provides a safe place to explore these feelings and emotions. When children play out troubling feelings and experiences, they learn how to deal with them. Play is a safe place to express feelings of hostility and aggression without resorting to physical violence or bullying. Feelings of powerlessness, fear, and sexual awakening often lead to aggression and violent acting out. For most children, playing provides an acceptable way for them to understand their negative feelings. For those children who are deeply disturbed, play offers one valuable tool to help adults understand what the child is going through.

Between the ages of five and seven, a child begins to develop empathy, that is, the ability to relate to the feelings of others. She knows that when she is hurt, she feels pain, and others feel the same when they are hurt. She knows that if she pulls the cat's tail, the cat will be hurt. This is an essential quality for healthy social development, and through play children have opportunities to nurture this capacity. Sociodramatic play encourages children to try on different roles to see how it feels to be someone else.

Play is also important as a means of releasing energy and aggression. Physical play, in particular, serves to diffuse excess energy and frustration and often prevents these feelings from degenerating into discipline problems. When children play fight they are practicing the age-old struggle for dominance. All animals have this instinct. If we watch puppies at play, we see them practicing strategies for self-preservation and dominance. But it is more than that. They are also learning how to control their impulses and use restraint. In play fighting, as opposed to real-life conflict, young animals do not go to the limits of their strength. It is much the same when older siblings or adults roughhouse with younger children. They play as if they were serious but hold back sufficiently to avoid harming the child.

Play also has the ability to calm a child and provide a needed distraction when things go wrong. As a child becomes absorbed in her play, she puts aside her fears and frustrations, and confidence is restored. The therapeutic aspects of play are particularly important for children who are experiencing stress.

In one of classrooms I visited on a regular basis, I came to know Lucas. He was the pawn in a messy divorce, and from one day to the next he didn't know where he would be living. Some mornings when he came into the kindergarten room, he headed for the sand or water table, and there he stayed sometimes for most of the morning. His teacher had the insight to know that Lucas needed this time and did not insist that he

133

come to the morning circle. This did not lead, by the way, to a mass revolution by other children who would have preferred to play. They too seemed to recognize Lucas's need.

At the sand table, Lucas calmed himself down, and we could visibly see the stress drain from his face. I have no doubt that had he had an authoritarian teacher who insisted that every child do the opening exercises as expected, this boy would have developed a serious discipline problem. As it was, play provided the respite he needed until he was able to cope with the demands of being in school.

When lack of self-discipline occurs during play, a child is dealt with by his peers but generally not to the detriment of self-esteem. Even when pushed out of the play for some inappropriate behavior, he is taken back when he changes that behavior. The consequences of his actions are clear to him.

If we establish the rules and trust our children, both the children and we ourselves will be relaxed and more productive. For play to exert its power, it must be free. Because children are free to play does not mean that play is chaos. It is important to the quality of play that children have clear boundaries for their behavior. As in all aspects of their lives, children need to have effective and consistent limits set by their parents and teachers.

The nature of the boundaries for play changes over time. As a child matures, she is able to assume increasingly more responsibility for her actions. A baby is driven by a tremendous force of will that is neither conscious nor under her control. She does not act in relationship to us, and cannot change simply because we insist. Through the preschool years, it is important for parents and teachers to remember this. When a child is difficult, it is all too easy for the parent and teachers to take it personally, as if the child were deliberately setting out to make life unpleasant. We need to be the adult and consider how unhappy the disruptive behavior is making the child. We need to find out why she is acting in an unsuitable way. This may require the help of a professional if things get too strained between the parent and child.

Rules are there to support play not hamper it. There are really only three external rules necessary for play:

- Could the child get hurt?

- Could someone else be harmed?

- Could there be serious damage?

These are essentially the rules for play. Most other considerations are unimportant.

What Can We Do To Help?

➢ Lighten up! Children have a wonderful capacity to thrive in the face of seemingly prohibitive obstacles. If we lighten up and take normal skirmishes in stride, we can reduce tension. Nothing defuses a potential outburst like a giggle. A humorous gesture or noise may be all it takes.

➢ Use your playfulness to get your child to behave appropriately. One young father I met while out shopping had a great solution. Keep the children entertained!

➢ Use the quick fix sparingly. There will be times in the course of everyday life when parents and teachers need to resort to a "quick fix," but it is important to keep in mind that imposing discipline at the expense of developing self-control is not an effective way to approach discipline. Disciplining children should always have the big picture in mind.

Being playful is a way of interacting with children both within play and in everyday life. It is an attitude toward children and play that creates a happy learning environment, minimizing power struggles and the day-to-day frustrations of parenting. Perhaps the most wonderful part of having children is sharing the joy of their play. Don't squander this experience by setting up unrealistic expectations and unnecessary power struggles. At each phase new rules and expectations can be established, but these should coincide with developmental characteristics. A two-year-old is not a four-year-old. A five-year-old is not a six-year-old, no matter how precocious the child seems. Relax and enjoy the wonderful gift of a child's play, and through it, find a magical means of leading your child toward autonomy.

10

Superhero and Aggressive Play: A Dilemma

Superhero play refers to the active, physical play of children pretending to be media characters imbued with extraordinary abilities, including superhuman strength or the ability to transform themselves into superhuman entities. While some view this play as violent and aggressive, it is not so by definition.

B. J. Boyd

Few aspects of children's play give parents and teachers more concern than superhero and aggressive play. For many of us, this concern is linked to the exposure of our children to rampant violence in the media. Over the past decade, there has been a dramatic increase in the amount of violence seen by young children on a daily basis through television and films. On the other hand, it is obvious to parents and teachers that superheroes and play fighting have a natural place in the world of play. Millions of children all over the world engage in play fighting and reenacting superhero adventures. Why is this? What needs does it satisfy?

Superheroes are the stuff of folk and fairy tales of bygone years. They provide a rich resource for pretend play. Superheroes are clearly differentiated into good and evil. Superheroes have superhuman powers that enable them to triumph over evil. They tend to be gruesome and filled with all manner of violent activities. For all of this, they have remained beloved favorites over the generations. Today's superheroes can be traced back to post World War I and the early days of comic books and cartoons. Superman, Batman, Wonder Woman, and Spiderman, to name a few, have endured through decades with each new audience as captivated as the earlier ones. Most recently the media figures of Ninja Turtles, Power Rangers, Pokemon, and the Star Wars heroes have emerged to join the list of favorites.

Why Children Need Superheroes

Why do children love these aggressive fantasies? What is it that they get from them? We tend to associate superheroes with violence and aggression, but as B. J. Boyd points out in the opening quote to this chapter, this is not necessarily the case. Superheroes feed the imagination and provide the wherewithal for lively pretend play. Superhero play is highly physical, and therefore it appeals to high-energy children who need to be on the move. We as adults may be more comfortable with the child who sits quietly than with the one who is leaping around using language that appears rude and unintelligible. In terms of learning, however, we need to go beyond the surface and think about what skills are being developed. It is more important *that* the children play than *what* they play. If during the episode of superhero play, the children must collaborate as they set off in search of the bad guys or try to rescue a victim, they will need communication skills. They will need to problem solve and to temper their aggression so as not to injure one another. On the other hand, the child sitting quietly may be missing out on some critical lessons from play.

In his book *Killing Monsters: Why Children Need Fantasy, Superheroes and Make-Believe Violence* (2002), Gerard Jones, a noted cartoonist and lecturer, reports on his extensive research on the topic. Jones interviewed psychiatrists, pediatricians, family therapists, teachers, and other parents. He concluded:

> The vast array of fantasies and stories we tend to dismiss with such labels as "media violence" are used well by children. I've seen young people turn every form of imaginary aggression into sources of emotional nourishment and developmental support.

Jones believes that adults tend to focus on the literal interpretation rather than the emotional meaning of stories and images. Even at a young age, most children can distinguish reality from fantasy. Children may appear to believe that the fantasy is real, but they know that they are not the Ninja Turtles or Spiderman.

Many years ago I was interviewed regarding the inclusion in a primary reader of a folk tale called "Mr. Miacca." This is the story about a little boy who doesn't do as he is told and as a result is captured by the sinister Mr. Miacca. As the story goes, Mr. Miacca is going to chop off the little boy's leg. Instead, he chops off a chair leg. Each time something dire is to happen, the boy outwits him. Adults thought this too gruesome for young children. The reporter believed that children would be frightened by this story. I had used this story with a number of grade-two classes and never found any evidence that children were anything but delighted with the tale. They appreciated the one-upmanship of the little boy. Seven-year-olds knew that this was fantasy and had no apparent trouble dealing with it. The story was removed from the reader to avoid complaints from parents and teachers. Too often the material we give to children to read or to view is so safe that no real issues are ever introduced.

Adults are often quick to place judgment on literature, films, music, and even behavior that reflects their own tastes and values rather than that of children. When adults hear children being rude to one another in superhero play, they treat this as if the child is being rude in real life, whereas he is acting out in role. Children know this and react differently when insulted during a play episode than when they are in the playground. These nasty spats are needed for children to figure out how to deal with interpersonal tension.

Some children are exposed to acts of violence in their home. They see their mom beaten and verbally abused. They may be the victims themselves. In some communities, children have firsthand knowledge of the consequences of violent actions. They see their brother or their cousin shot in a gang dispute. They hear about a neighbor who has been beaten up. If not firsthand, children are more than aware of the violence in society from newscasts and reality shows. Children tend to respond to violence by acting it out. They may get out the toy soldiers or pretend to be involved in a shootout. This is their way of trying to understand what is going on. They play with what's troubling them in order to feel safe. Psychologists (Weininger 1982) tell us that if aggression does not come out in play, it will probably come out in storytelling, painting, or some other form of communication.

Chart 10.1

BENEFITS OF SUPERHERO PLAY	
Requires high energy	An important avenue for high energy children to expend some of their energy Is an excellent way to gain physical benefits from the running, jumping, tumbling of this play
Has universal appeal	Children of all cultures play superheroes, reflecting those that are a reflection of their own myths
Explores universal themes	The themes found in literature, in particular good versus evil, death and rebirth, are at the heart of superhero play. These themes are as old as mankind.
Helps to work through anxiety, fear and feelings of helplessness	Superhero play is a safe place to play out difficult emotions and find ways of dealing with them.

Aggression in Play

Aggression is an expression of the need to feel in control, to feel powerful. It is a response to deeply felt anger. Adults tend to be uncomfortable with children's anger. We would prefer to think of their lives as worry free and happy, when in reality for many children this is a myth. Too many children are gripped by fear, anger, and hopelessness. Is it any wonder that their aggression gets out of hand? Children who hurt others, bully younger children, and cause intentional damage are not playing. These children mix rough and tumble with real aggression that too quickly can escalate from playful fighting to destructive aggression.

Destructive aggression is simply violence, and if not stopped, will only lead to greater violence. It is important for an adult to step in and help a child cool down, either by holding him or giving him breathing room. One of the worst things we can do is to isolate the child by time-out. The child needs the safety of a caring adult, not further isolation and feelings of failure. Time-out may be a necessary strategy when a child is out of control, but an adult should be with him to provide some sense of security. Children who are too angry to play safely are likely to need professional intervention.

Rough and tumble is one form of aggressive play that parents and teachers tend to discourage. It is noisy and can get out of hand, quickly leading to head bumping and tears. For all of that, rough and tumble has a number of important benefits. Rough and tumble play helps to

- provide physical exercise,

- hone social skills,

- manage and defuse anxiety and frustration, and

- give children practice in healthy competition.

If you are uncomfortable with superhero play, you need to take time to listen and observe what your children are doing. In an article, *Coping with Ninja Turtle Play in My Kindergarten Classroom* (1992), Gaye Gronlund describes the problems she had as a teacher with children repeatedly playing superhero characters. As uncomfortable as she was with this play, she could not ignore the fascination the children had for the Ninja Turtles. Once she relaxed and decided to find out more about the Ninja Turtles, she discovered that there was value to the play in spite of the limited themes. While she remained unconvinced that such superheroes should be part of children's fantasies, she saw the value in using these kinds of media fantasies as a means of helping children explore the nature of violence and aggression. She reminds us that if we don't know the characters and the plots, we need to watch these programs with children. We need to ask the children to tell us about these characters. Children love to be able to explain things to you, and that in itself will defuse much of the aggression.

I had a similar situation in a grade-one classroom that I visited on a regular basis. The teacher had a wonderful writing program, and I followed the children's progress from mainly invented spelling to some amazingly mature writing. Three little boys, all of whom were quite advanced in their writing, seemed almost obsessed with Ninja Turtles. The teacher was not sure whether to let them write what they chose, as was the practice in this program, or to forbid them to write about Ninja Turtles. From time to time, she gave these boys a different topic, and they wrote about what she had asked. But these stories lacked the humor, detail, and elaborate sentence structure of their Ninja stories. We watched these children for months, and they never lost their enthusiasm for these little reptiles.

I happened to be in the school early in the following September. I was interested to see what they were writing about now that they were in second grade. "You're going to be sorry," said one of the little boys. "I'm not making stories anymore about Ninja Turtles." He had moved on, but the skills he honed writing these countless adventures featuring Ninja Turtles allowed him to remain well above others of a similar age.

As with pretend play, the content is not nearly as important as learning through the process. This was an excellent learning experience for the classroom teacher and me as we realized that no harm had come from respecting a child's choice of topic for writing.

Aggressive Play and the Media: Two Views

Closely bound to issues of aggression in play is the perception of the effects of the media on this aggression. There is no consensus on whether aggression in the media has a negative effect on play. On one hand, there are those who claim that violence in the media has a negative effect on children's play behavior and permeates their development.

This view sees the negative influence in objectionable language and actions that come out in their play. They see children being disrespectful of one another and abusive. They see the children imitating physical violence rather than using language to resolve a conflict. In her book *Remote Control Childhood*, Diane Levin (1998) states:

Media violence and other aspects of media culture are a public health issue that affects us all. Professionals trained to care about the well-being of children and society—among them the American Academy of Pediatrics, the American Medical Association, the American Psychological Association, the National Association for the Education of Young Children, the National Parent-Teacher Association, and the U.S. Surgeon General and Attorney General—have begun saying enough is enough..

Ten years later, things haven't changed very much. Canada has stricter guidelines in place than those in the United States, but the proliferation of online media, in particular pornography, exploiting children makes the concerns almost overwhelming.

The concerns of those who believe that violence in the media has a negative effect on children can be summed up as follows:

- Children are seduced into inactivity by TV and computer games. Instead of engaging in physical play, they are sedentary and at risk of obesity and other physical problems associated with inactivity.

- Stories and characters are stereotypical, following a formula that erodes creativity. There is nothing in these stories to inspire the imagination. They project the images of the worst stereotypes. Boys are macho beings who fight at the drop of a hat. Girls are helpless twits who sit around and wait to get rescued. Attempts have been made to reverse these images, but on the whole they remain entrenched in popular TV and film.

- Various studies suggest that children exposed to popular culture for extended amounts of time absorb the undesirable values portrayed in much of today's entertainment.

• The introduction of Internet culture into homes has brought with it the potential for unprecedented exploitation of children. The escalation of online child pornography is frightening.

• Through gimmicks designed to lure children into giving out personal information, there is an unprecedented invasion of children's privacy. With the promise of a free T-shirt or some other prize, children are enticed into filling out questionnaires that provide personal information. This same ploy is used when they sign on to play some interactive games or join some chat rooms. Unscrupulous people have blurred the lines between advertising and play. Children think they are playing, but there is much more going on.

Those who see entertainment aggression as a serious negative influence believe that media violence affects both what children play and how they play. In terms of what they play, media entertainment prompts themes of good and bad guys with actions that are limited to scenes of fighting. In terms of how they play, the episodes are less complex and the characters stereotypical. The process of sociodramatic play involves creating roles, a set of actions, and language around a theme, usually reflecting life as they experience it. When children enact episodes of violence from the media, they are likely to rework the same limited set of actions and roles. Language is confined to this narrow sequence of actions. In replaying action programs, the play is limited mainly to the standard chasing and car crashes. The actions rarely develop into any kind of extension. Given these observations, there appear to be legitimate reasons for banishing this type of play.

On the other hand are those who view aggression in the media as much less harmful than has been suggested. While exposure to aggression in the media may result in play that is less creative, it does not seem to cause aggressive behavior later on in childhood and adolescence. Gerald Jones (2002), for example, questions the very studies that often are cited as proof of the negative influences. He suggests that many of the studies condemning media violence are based on flawed research. He points out that in some studies no distinction was made between play aggression and violent behavior. In some of these studies, acts of violence might be anything from a small push to a vicious attack with a baseball bat. Jones also found that researcher bias was evident in analysis of the data. The researchers tended to see what they wanted to see.

The fact that the themes, roles, and actions of sociodramatic play based on television are limited and often stereotypical is a legitimate concern and one that should be addressed. Rather than banning all such play, it will be more effective to present children with other options, to extend by suggestion, or to become a player and unobtrusively redirect the actions.

The use of guns in superhero play can also be troubling. Parents and teachers see the use of guns as symbolic of violent behavior in real life. By permitting children to play fight with pretend guns, we are afraid that we may be condoning violence. No matter how hard we try, however, the struggle to ban pretend guns is a losing battle. Gun play is universal, and in the absence of a replica gun, children are ingenious in using other props—their fingers, a stick, and so on. Sometimes guns are a form of magic wand to the young child. The gun gives power and control. It can destroy, but it also can bring life back. The important thing for adults is to watch what the children are doing with the gun. Is it an enactment of violence from the media, or is it in fact simply a form of magic?

The conflicting views on the effects of the media are confusing for parents and teachers. Should we ban it all together? Should we encourage it? A master of education candidate, Diane McQuay-Sellwood (1998), found herself in the position as a kindergarten teacher of having to enforce a no superhero/guns policy in her classroom. Her frustration led her to conduct a research study in her classroom to examine the nature of superhero play and how it affected general behavior. When she designed her study, she deliberately chose to be a nonparticipant observer using videotapes for data collection. In her conclusions, McQuay-Sellwood notes that she did not find the children's play to be as noisy, aggressive, or out of control as the literature had suggested. She found a number of positive effects of superhero play.

- Superheroes provide a sure-fire means of capturing the interest of little boys who are difficult to reach. The innate fascination with superhero play is a powerful way of motivating them.

- Superhero play offers a means of helping children move from the familiar rituals and roles of family to more imaginative worlds and exploring themes beyond family.

- Superhero play provides opportunity for reciprocal give and take between playmates. It supports social development as children learn to control their impulses and moderate their aggression to accommodate others.

- Superhero play promotes physical activity and encourages flexibility and strength. This leads to confidence and self-awareness. This is particularly important for children who may not be as mature in language and social skills as others.

While it is clear from these conflicting views that not all superhero play is harmful, and that rich, energetic play may be the result, it is also clear that there are very legitimate reasons for us to be concerned. We need to distinguish between the superhero play that most children enjoy and the reenactment of violent, stereotypical characters. Superheroes such as Superman or Spiderman are fantasy characters that clearly set out good and evil. In these adventures, good prevails and evil is punished. The villains are not elevated to the stature of hero, but are shown for what they are. In other contemporary superhero characters, we find the opposite. Rudeness is the norm, the hero is often the villain, and children are left with the belief that it doesn't matter what you do to win, it's winning that counts.

If we are to make sound judgments about superhero play, we need to put aside our own distaste for particular superheroes and stereotypical programs and recognize that every generation has its own popular culture and that each successive generation looks on the next as depraved. This is not to say that as custodians of today's children we ought not to speak out against the insidious intrusion of inappropriate heroes and activities that rob them of their innocence and rich play worlds.

Chart 10.2

SUPERHERO PLAY: WHAT TO LOOK FOR
Superhero play can be a rich resource for pretending. When it is used this way, both good and bad characters are imagined and the play is obviously satisfying. Superheroes, however, can be a vehicle for unhealthy aggression and bullying. When this happens, parents and teachers should watch carefully and use the opportunity to provide constructive intervention. The answer is not to forbid the play. This simply will lead to the aggression and bullying taking on a different face. It is better to join in and mediate between the children when necessary. If it is getting out of hand, you may consider looking for professional help.

Pretend Superhero Play	*Aggressive Play*
Are the children having fun?	Is there anger and tension among the children?
Are they exuberant?	Are their actions agitated and frenzied?
Are they careful not to hurt one another?	Do they seem to use the play to bully other children?
Is the aggression obviously pretend?	Does the aggression appear to be for real?
Do they use weapons as magic wands as well as a means of destruction?	Are the weapons always ones that do harm?

We need to select toys that will capture the child's imagination. If a child insists on action figures, supplement these with other props that will encourage the children to go beyond the limited few actions of the original stories.

A teacher friend of mine felt very strongly about the stereotyping and aggression in the superhero play going on in her classroom. She tried a number of things to discourage the play but to no avail. Children were not allowed to bring their action figures into the classroom. She found them tucked away in coat pockets to be taken out during outdoor play. Finally, in exasperation she decided to try the opposite tactic, that is, she set up a theme based on superheroes. The children were delighted. They brought in their favorite action figures, the girls as well as the boys, and she used these figures to discuss such themes as respect, helping one another, and so on. She led the children toward understanding the difference between good superheroes and bad ones. Like McQuay-Sellwood, she found that there was very little if any violence in their superhero play and that often, it became simply an episode of family with the characters being superheroes.

In order to make effective judgments, we need to learn to be astute observers. What are they doing with the heroes? Is their boisterousness the result of excitement or is it escalating anger? Are their conflicts part and parcel of young children learning how to get along, or are they bullying? As far as possible, we have to let children regulate their own play, intervening only when someone is going to get hurt or something damaged. When the children look to you to resolve their conflicts, encourage them to do so for themselves

Danny came over to his teacher complaining that Luke would not let him be Spiderman.

"He always plays Spiderman. I never get to be anybody good."

"Have you told Luke how you feel?" asked his teacher.

Danny goes over to Luke and says, "Mr. Benson says you gotta let me be Spiderman."

"Well," said Luke, "just this once," as he relinquished the cape.

This was not quite what the teacher had suggested, but Danny ended up solving his own problem without further confrontation.

We need to remember that games involving chasing, pillow fighting, squirt guns, and mock combat help children learn how to judge dangers and take appropriate risks. They also teach children how to adjust their own physical aggression to avoid harm to younger or weaker children.

While I don't suggest that we actively encourage superhero play, we can reduce the likelihood of having superheroes dominate children's play by discouraging unlimited TV and video games. In terms of television, we need to take on the role of media police by

- limiting access and exposure to the amount of time spent watching TV or playing computer games,

- monitoring the content,

- and making sure you know what your children are watching. Have you ever sat through an episode of your child's favorite program? What is your child watching at his friend's home? Is it monitored?

In terms of the viewing habits of your children, it is never too early to encourage good media habits. If children grow up with limits on how much as well as what they can watch on TV, they will see this as an expectation as they grow older. Take an active role in teaching your children to be discriminating in what they watch. It is also important that you are a role model for your children. Let them see you doing outdoor activities such as gardening, taking a walk, or going to the community pool. If children see their parent plunked down in front of the TV at every opportunity, the message is clear!

> *Experts suggest that two hours of TV a day is a sensible average. There is no magic number, however, and there are occasions, particularly when these involve a program enjoyed by the whole family, that the amount of time is stretched.*

> *Experts also suggest that there should not be a TV or computer in the child's room. Place it in a spot where the whole family has access.*

Issues of superhero play, aggression, and the media will not go away anytime soon. Today's children are growing up in a world vastly different from that of their parents. The exposure today's children have to depravity and violence is alarming. As adults we have a serious responsibility to protect them from the insidious erosion of innocence. The mind of a child ought not to be polluted with the unhealthy images presented in the media. Such images will have an impact on their play as they try to understand what they see. Whether it is violence in the home or on a screen, the consequences are the same: a reduction in the quality of play, and therefore, in the power it has to stimulate development and learning.

What Can We Do To Help?

➢ Don't be afraid of superhero play. There are many good things that come from this play, including the ability to control the level of aggression in play.

➢ If superhero play seems to be just a reworking of a few acts of aggression, like the car crash and the karate kicks, introduce something to divert children's interest in extending the play. You may need to join in to do this and use your own imagination to come up with an appealing idea.

➢ Be alert to your child's use of electronic games and other forms of passive entertainment. All children need an escape, just as adults do. However, when these games or programs become a substitute for doing other things, then there is cause for concern.

Children use aggressive fantasies for several purposes. When they play superhero, they have feelings of power, something they rarely experience elsewhere. This helps them to control their emotions and perhaps work through anxieties that they cannot yet put a voice to. Superhero play, contrary to what we might believe, can actually calm children down with the release of energy needed for this play. This is particularly so of the overly exuberant child. It is a safe way to get rid of anger, while at the same time allowing the child to learn how to control his aggression.

Among the many fantasy roles that children take on in their play are good guys and bad guys. Once known as cops and robbers, this kind of play is now more likely to involve superheroes or fantasy characters from TV and movies. The main thing for parents to remember about this type of play is that it is not as destructive or as horrid as it may seem. Superhero or good guy/bad guy play is a human way of practicing control over aggression.

Lawrence Cohen

Part 3

Back to Basics:

Learning Naturally

Many adults in our society still think of education in terms of intellectual development and see the work of the schools as preparation for achievement in examinations, leading to a career...

When facts and procedures, memorized for examination purposes, have been forgotten, the final product of education is the sort of person that is left.

Alice Yardley

11

Play and the Basics

As we know from investigations of the process of concept formation, a concept is more than the sum of certain associative bonds formed by memory, more than a mere mental habit; it is a complex and genuine act of thought that cannot be taught by drilling but can be accomplished only when the child's mental development itself has reached a requisite level. Practical experience also shows that direct teaching of concepts is impossible and fruitless. A teacher who tries to do this usually accomplishes nothing but empty verbalism, a parrot-like repetition of words by the child, simulating a knowledge of corresponding concepts but actually covering up a vacuum.

Lev Vygotsky

Over the past decade the "back to the basics" movement has strongly influenced the policy and practice of public education. Emphasis on academic knowledge and skills, particularly in the areas of reading and mathematics, has pushed aside play. Parents are finding that preschools and childcare, not to mention kindergartens, are not exempt from the pressure to ramp up math and reading instruction. More rigorous attention to basic academics is in response to the pressure for accountability, the competitive marketplace, and the shifting global economy.

Education is an expensive endeavor. Society has the right to ask, what are we getting for our dollars and how do we know? In order to ensure that "no child is left behind," steps are being taken to provide a firm foundation in the early years for academic success. Reading receives particular attention, with a return to phonics in many jurisdictions, as the way to introduce children to reading. Standardized tests are being used as early as kindergarten to address the accountability issue. Many parents, wanting to provide a leg up for their child in terms of school success, welcome these changes.

Taking the early years seriously is a major breakthrough in education, but in order to build a foundation for school success, we must resolve two questions:

- What are the basics?

- How do children learn the basics?

When we resolve these two questions, we can begin to make serious inroads into providing better beginnings for our children.

Basics for the Twenty-First Century

To begin with, we need to clearly identify the basics. As important as reading and math are to success in life, at the very least we need to consider *the four Rs* – reading, writing, arithmetic, and *the Arts*. Music, visual art, dance, and drama are fundamental ways of communicating. They express our deepest emotions and passions. They provide a means of releasing the imagination. To be an artist is to be uniquely human. Many studies support the claim that the arts have an important role in shaping the development of the intellect. The arts are not simply a diversion but a vital part of human development. To ignore the arts as a fundamental human need is to deprive our children of one of life's greatest joys. How indeed can we speak of an educated person while treating the arts as trivial?

In addition to the four Rs, there is ample indication that what have come to be called the *employability skills* for the new economy are vital to personal fulfillment as well as the economic growth of our society. The Conference Board of Canada, a not-for-profit applied research organization that concerns itself with, among other things, economic trends and public policy, has for some time argued that the employability skills needed for today's changing job market must include personal management skills and teamwork skills as well as academic skills. Similar skills have been described by organizations around the world as the marketplace skills of tomorrow. SkillsUSA, a nonprofit organization devoted to developing a skilled workforce, identifies communication, problem solving, teamwork, and self-management as the employability skills for the new economy.

These employability skills are not job specific but can be used in any type of employment. This is different from many technical skills that can be applied to only one specific job. Workers who have only technical skills are ones who can do one particular job but cannot adapt when a problem arises or the need to change jobs occurs.

The workplace of today is already different from that of the past generation. The expectation that one would stay in the same job for life and perhaps even in the same company is no longer viable. Companies come and go. Traditional jobs disappear and new ones open up. What this adds up to is a new set of skills that equip the next generation with flexibility of mind, the ingenuity to be a self-starter, as well as the self-confidence and humility to work effectively with others. Tomorrow's employees will need to be adaptable as they move from one job to another, from one location to another. They will need to have energy and optimism in order to make a positive contribution to resolving serious global problems. Technology has taken over some of the more mundane skills we taught religiously in schools. Computers can spell check and do complicated mathematical operations in seconds. The human brain is designed for much greater things.

Another basic skill for the twenty-first century is that of *ecological literacy*, that is, the basics about the earth and how it works. The growing awareness that ecological changes and sustainability are the new challenges that face humanity has become a reality. David Orr in his book Ecological Literacy(1992) states that:

> If literacy is driven by the search for knowledge, ecological literacy is driven by a sense of wonder, the sheer delight in being alive in a beautiful, mysterious, bountiful world. The darkness and disorder we have brought to the world give ecological literacy an urgency it lacked a century ago. We can now look over the abyss and see the end of it all. Ecological literacy begins in childhood.

> *Marketplace Skills for the New Economy*
>
> *Academic Skills*
> > *Communication*
> > *Thinking*
> > *Lifelong learning*
>
> *Personal Management Skills*
> > *Positive attitudes and behaviors*
> > *Responsibility*
>
> *Teamwork*
> > *Negotiate*
> > *Collaborate*
> > *Communicate*
>
>
>
> *Conference Board of Canada*
> *255 Smyth Road*
> *Ottawa, On. Canada*
> *K1H 8M7*
>
>

Ecological literacy is about relatedness: how the various elements of the earth relate to one another and how we relate to the earth and to each another. This is an inquiring approach to education that stands at the opposite end of memorizing formulas and facts that are being disproved as fast as schools promote them. Ecological literacy is born of play and the search for meaning.

Learning the Basics Naturally through Play

Traditionally, direct instruction has been the main method used for instruction in schools. While experience-based learning has been around for over half a century, much of our educational practice, from planning to assessment, is based on a notion of directed instruction using step-by-step lessons. This works for low-level skills, but when it comes to higher levels of thinking, this simplistic approach does not work. The brain is much too active and multifaceted to operate this way.

This brings us back to the business of play and learning. As we have discussed throughout this book, play provides an unprecedented opportunity to develop all of the personal and teamwork skills described by the Conference Board of Canada, SkillsUSA, and other organizations. Endorsing play as a means of developing the arts, employability skills, and ecological literacy does not negate the place of directed instruction in learning, but simply suggests that for young children, play offers the most effective and lasting means of establishing a foundation for all of these skills.

Spontaneous Learning or Directed Instruction

At some point in time, children will benefit from directed instruction, but spontaneous learning through play is the foundation upon which all of the rest lies. It should not come down to a competition between directed instruction and spontaneous learning through play. Rather, we should respect the power of play in learning, and introduce systematic, directed instruction as the mind becomes ready to accept what is being offered and when what is to be learned can efficiently be presented in a sequential series of tasks. A violinist needs to have technical skills in order to create exquisite music. A scientist has to have many technical skills in order to pursue yet unimagined solutions for global problems. If the violinist or the scientist has only technical skill, not only does she miss out on being the best she can be, but the world misses out by not having her contribution. Technique is important but no more so than creativity.

We've got it wrong when, in the guise of back to the basics, we push down directed instruction into kindergarten and preschool at the cost of learning through play. What we must do is push play up through the primary grades, the middle years, and beyond.

In preschool and kindergarten, spontaneous learning through play should be the norm, and as children mature, directed instruction should increase so that by the middle grades, both spontaneous learning and directed learning have a place. This would allow the best possible way of addressing the broad range of marketable knowledge and skills. By incorporating play alongside directed instruction in the middle and upper grades, we make it possible for children to learn basic skills while at the same time nurturing the confidence, imagination, and perseverance to thrive in an ever-changing world.

It has always been a puzzle to me, having seen the way babies and toddlers learn with joy and ease through play, that by virtue of crossing the doorstep of a place called school, they are suddenly thought to learn best through teacher-directed lessons. The two most stunning human achievements—learning to talk and learning to walk—are done without directed instruction. In fact, the psycholinguist Kenneth Goodman once remarked that if we taught talking the way we teach reading, our schools would be filled with remedial talking classes. These two complex accomplishments come about through free, self-directed learning.

Through play in preschool and kindergarten, children spontaneously acquire the profound notion of quantity, causality, time, and space, as well as a host of other fundamental understandings about the world. The core of the argument between learning through play and learning through a prescribed set of lessons is the difference between focusing on learning versus teaching. When the mind is ready, it can benefit from instruction but the only way to ready it is through play. It is in the balancing of spontaneous learning through play and directed learning through instruction that the true artistry of being a teacher can be found.

What Can We Do To Help?

> ➤ Recognize that the marketplace of tomorrow will be very different from what we've known. Many of the traditional jobs have already disappeared, and new ones that reflect the changing face of employment are taking their place. As parents and as teachers, we need to nurture the skills basic to the changing world—flexibility, adaptability, creativity, and communication. We need to build confidence, initiative,

curiosity, and risk-taking in our children so that they will thrive in the world of tomorrow.

➤ Instill a sense of wonder at the amazing planet earth. Make conservation and respect for the creatures of the earth a given in your household.

➤ Foster a social conscience in your young child. He will grow up in the global society of tomorrow where barriers of culture and race will disappear in the intermingling of people around the globe.

Through play, children learn what they need, when they need it without the intrusion of instruction. Play is the best possible way children have of developing a solid foundation for the new basics.

There's more to learning than counting to ten or the ABCs.

12

Bringing Children and Reading Together through Play

It is important to introduce young children to poems, songs, jingles and rhymes as early in life as possible... Poetry and songs build a child's awareness of rhythm and rhyme and bring pattern and shape to print. Adults can sing or read the poem aloud, or share it with children as they read together.

David Booth and Bill Moore

Parents are well aware that reading is fundamental to all of the new basics. What we may not understand is how important play is to language and ultimately reading development. But before we look at the connections between play and reading, we need to be clear about how children learn to read.

Reading Begins at Home

Parents generally think that learning the alphabet is the first step toward reading. Reading, however, begins long before this with the first glimmers of language. Learning how to read is like learning how to talk. Children learn talk by being surrounded by talk. We talk to our babies all the time, even though we realize that their capacity to understand what we say is limited. Babies hear talk all day long in conversations around the home and on television. No one teaches a baby about grammar or worries that the first modest attempts at talk are not yet conventional. We don't panic if the pace of learning to talk is different from one child to another. We see the individual developmental timetable at work in all aspects of our child's growth.

Reading is a similar process. Babies are introduced to reading through storybooks. We have known for a long time that reading to babies is an important first step on the journey to literacy. And what is it that babies and toddlers learn from having stories read to them? To begin with, they learn important features of a book. A book has a front and back. Words are written from left to right. The story moves from the left hand page to the right and from the top to the bottom. All of this comes from watching as Mom or Dad opens the book, turns the pages, shows the baby the pictures, and points out other things of interest.

Children also learn how events move in a sequence as well as the difference between the sound of talk and the sound of written language. There is a rhythm and flow to written language that makes it sound quite different from spoken language. We never, for example, go up to someone and say, "once upon a time," but many children's stories begin with this phrase. In fact, when children first begin to write their own stories, they often rely on this phrase, as well as "the end" to mark the boundaries of their narrative.

Perhaps one of the most important lessons of this early story time is the feeling of closeness and delight caught from the intimate moments of being read to by a parent or other loved one. Those of us fortunate enough to have had parents who read to us can still experience the warmth, as I do after all these years, of cuddling up with my father on a blustery winter's Sunday afternoon listening to my favorite stories. It didn't matter whether it was the comics, a story he made up, or one of my favorites, *The Tales of Peter Rabbit*. The experience is what has stayed with me. Children are not conscious of learning these things, but they initiate a child into reading.

Parents don't have to know all about the reading process in order to nurture reading; they simply need to immerse their children in books and stories and have them become actively involved. We might have the child turn the page, point to something interesting, guess what might be going to happen next, and so on. Reading in the preschool years should be a playful, relaxed experience with the child having some control over what is read to him, deciding when to pause and even when to stop if he has lost interest.

Having provided many stories to our children and perhaps having built a library of personal favorites, we are tempted to assume that our children will be ready for reading instruction when they start school.

Like all development, however, reading develops in its own time and at its own pace. Some children will begin to read on their own by age five and others not until as late as eight years of age. Many children who go on to become excellent readers may not read independently until well into the primary grades.

Dennis was in my grade-one classroom. His parents, who were both avid readers, were very concerned when half way through grade one he was not reading. They spent all weekend reading the pre-primer with him and, of course, Dennis soon had it memorized.

I can recall the look of excitement on Dennis's face as he proudly announced on Monday morning, "Look, I can read my book." He stood up and read the first pre-primer with all the expression of a good reader. The only giveaway was that he held the book upside down.

I explained to his parents that Dennis, for whatever reason, was not at the place where he could benefit from instruction. He needed more time and experience. I encouraged them to continue reading to him and being patient until all of the necessary development was in place. It was toward the end of grade two that he fell into reading. To their credit, Dennis's parents kept faith in him and were rewarded by Dennis turning into a genuine bookworm. The important thing is for the child to remain confident that in his own time, he will be successful.

Scandinavian countries, among the most literate nations in the world, have long recognized that waiting until a child is seven to begin instruction pays dividends in the long run. Children learn much faster and with pleasure. The Waldorf schools, founded on the principles set out by Rudolph Steiner, allow children to take their time and consider a child who begins to read in third grade quite normal.

The ability to read early is not an indicator of superior intelligence. Many "late bloomers" go on to make significant contributions to society. In my experience children who begin later than first grade can easily overtake the early readers by the end of the primary grades. The danger in pushing too early is that this often results in the erosion of confidence and a deeply rooted dislike of reading.

Chart 12.1

ON THE WAY TO READING	
What to Look For	**Resources**
0-1 year • Mainly interested in pictures and sounds of the language	• Picture Books • Nursery Rhymes • All kinds of poetry and prose • Books for babies - cloth and board books • Begin your child's personal collections of books

1-3 years
• Begin to notice features of the book, that is, books written in English are read from:
  o Front to back
  o Top to bottom
  o One page after another from left to right
• Begin to have distinct favorites that must be read over and over again
	• Picture Books
	• Pop-up books & ones with interesting features
	• Regular visits to the community library for story time and borrowing books
	• Add favorites to his collection
	• Around age two, may want to simply point to details on each page

3-6 years
• Engage in pretend reading using inflection and expression as if truly reading
• Begins to notice words and develop a sight vocabulary of frequently used words
• Begin to develop the skill of predicting:
  o What might happen next
  o What the next word might be
• Begin to recognize letters of the alphabet and notice features that make a difference p *p* p
	• A wide variety of picture books
	• Books that the child and parent create together

5-8 years • Children will begin to read independently • They may go through a period in which they move in and out of interest particularly in the beginning.	• Recognize that already your child will have preferences about the kind of books she likes • This is a good time to get a magazine subscription in his name

Literacy through Play

As noted in chapter 4, the connections between play and literacy have been a topic of many research studies over the past several decades. We know that by virtue of the fact that play, in particular pretend play, has such an important role in developing oral language, it also strengthens the development of reading. Play stimulates the imagination, another essential ingredient for reading.

In addition to these indirect influences, play supports reading through directly addressing two central aspects of story:

- Character and plot—constructing characters and events from bits and pieces of everyday life

- Dialogue—recognizing that different settings call for different ways of talking; that people have different ways of speaking

Children naturally bring reading into their sociodramatic play. I've seen many examples like the following one.

Five-year-old Henrique is playing hospital with three of his friends. He is stretched out on the cot with a doll tucked under his arm. The nurse has been feeding him a pretend meal made of wooden cubes. She tires of care giving and announces:

"Come on, guys, let's go shopping."

Just as they are about to leave, Henrique is heard to call, "Nurse, nurse. I need some books to read to my baby."

Monica, the nurse, goes over to the library and selects several picture books that she brings over to him.

Henrique is then seen play reading to his "baby," showing the pictures as he goes. When I shared this anecdote with Henrique's parents, they were delighted and somewhat surprised at how important story time was to him.

Writing also is brought into sociodramatic play. A young child first uses writing to make a shopping list, a greeting card, or a message, all of which are very important to young children.

During an episode of restaurant, five-year-old Lee and I are seated at a small table set for a meal. Five-year-old Brendan, who is the waiter, picks up a note pad and a magic marker.

"What would you like for your dinner?" Brendan asks.

I hesitate for a few seconds to consider what to say.

"Hurry up. I don't have all day, you know!" says Brendan sharply.

"How about lamb chops and chocolate pie?" I reply.

"Make that two lamb chops!" Lee chimes in.

"Two lamb chops coming up," Brendan replies.

The order is written on the notepad in invented spelling.

After the orders are brought, a bill is written up and presented to us.

This episode shows that the children already know that the circumstances determine both what is said and how it is said. This brief dialogue sounds like a restaurant conversation. It also shows that these children understand that information can be written down, and although they do not yet have the skills of conventional spelling, this does not stop them from "playing" with language.

We can encourage our children to include reading and writing in their play by making the necessary resources available. Books, pencils, markers, crayons, paper of various sizes and colors should be accessible and sometimes out on display in the play area to remind children of the possibilities for reading and writing while at play.

When being a play partner, we can model the use of literacy and suggest ways of including reading and writing. If, for instance, the children are planning a birthday party for their dollies, we might suggest that they make invitations. Recipients of the invitations can respond in writing, and this in turn provides an authentic use for both reading and writing through the children's play.

As children mature, literacy becomes an integral part of playing games. In the early stages, age three and four, pictures on a board game provide clues to what should be done. Later on reading and interpreting rules will become very important. When playing a board game, point out how to "read" the picture clues on the board (e.g., How do you know where to begin? How do you know where the finish line is?). Card games such as lotto help children to see similarities and differences in objects, and later on, letters of the alphabet and words.

Conversation is an important ingredient in learning to read, even if it's with a pretend friend.

There are many opportunities for parents and teachers to introduce literacy into play. We must not forget, however, that play is important in and of itself. The risk we face in schools when we think about literacy as a part of play in kindergarten and grade one is that literacy will take over and replace play. I do not think I have read a more articulate description of this problem than the following one written by Brenda Grandinetti, an exceptional kindergarten teacher, in an article she co-authored with me.

I have always been interested in literacy and love to share my enthusiasm for reading with children. From my earliest days as a primary teacher, I placed great value in helping children learn to read. I chose each book for story time as though it were a treasure and took pride in the way the children responded to my invitations to participate.

As time passed, I found it increasingly difficult to resist the movement to teach literacy at the expense of play. I introduced process writing, shared reading, and a borrow-a-book program in my classroom. I was pleased with what I saw, but doubts gnawed at me as I observed children struggling to meet my expectations and noticed that dramatic play, indeed, play of all kinds, had begun to diminish. As I looked for clues as to why this was happening, I noticed that my home center, always an area of rich imaginative play in the past, had shrunk to a bachelor-size apartment. This had been necessary since the computer cord was quite short, and I needed space to accommodate the writing center.

The whole issue really came to a head the day the beans went missing. On that morning, as I moved from one activity to another, I picked up the empty bean container from the floor where it had been discarded. Like Jack's, these were no ordinary beans. After a workshop on "activity mathematics," I had been inspired to purchase a kilogram of white kidney beans and spray one side of each bright green. These beans were guaranteed to provide material for counting, sorting, and a variety of other mathematical experiences. Now they had disappeared.

Nearby children were playing in the home center. Erin, wrapped in a lace curtain with a gold crown perched atop her head, was stirring a large pot on the stove—a pot which upon closer inspection contained an assortment of crayons, seashells, and the missing beans.

168

"Are you staying for dinner?" Erin asked. "We're having three-bean salad."

Shortly after the session with the beans, I attended a workshop on "whole language" for kindergarten teachers. Following the workshop, I made this entry in my journal:

"I listen carefully as an expert describes how to teach literacy in kindergarten. Many of the ideas are familiar to me. All are based on holistic principles of language and learning that I strongly endorse. Nonetheless, I am beginning to feel uncomfortable, but I don't know why. There is nothing here with which I disagree. What is bothering me about this program? Then I realize what it is. The program being described would be wonderful for seven- and eight-year-olds. Is it essential that five-year-olds be taught to read and write? Does this make children avid readers later on? What about play? Nudging children toward reading and writing has always been an acceptable practice in kindergarten, but this is no longer nudging. It has quickly become an expectation for all children."

Brenda went on from this point to develop a wonderfully balanced approach to early education that placed play at the center, while instilling a love of reading in her young students.

Parents and teachers who share a love of reading with their children, and who work together to make sure that children have the best of picture books from which to read, cannot go wrong.

Learning to Read or Teaching to Read: A Footnote

Reading to children and encouraging them to include reading and writing in their play may seem too simple to parents concerned with getting their child off to a solid start. The problem is the tradition of *reading readiness*. This is the basis for the idea that the alphabet comes first, then words, and then sentences. At this point, usually in grade one, we began formal reading instruction.

What of the illiterate parent or the teen mom who has limited reading skills? Recognizing how important it is for children to have parents who can read, communities and individuals around the country try to address this issue through a number of different programs. One such program, Literature for Life, has been established in Toronto for teen moms to help build skills, self-esteem, and aspirations. As Barbara Turnbull, author of an article that appeared in the *Toronto Star* September 2005, writes, "When a young mother learns to love reading, it changes two lives."

The founder of the Literature for Life initiative is a former teacher and mother of three who has invested countless volunteer hours in the project. Book groups are held at several locations in conjunction with community agencies. The participants discuss books, share views, and are encouraged to keep a personal journal. A newsletter, *Yo'Mama*, written and produced by volunteers from the participants, gives a voice to young women too often left powerless.

Programs like these open doors for mothers and their children. The investment of time and energy is substantial on the part of those who run the program. The group has received some funding from a local foundation and an organization for crime prevention. This is the type of program that can make a huge difference.

For over a century, one method after another has been contrived to teach children how to read. The earliest methods relied on sight words and/or phonics. These methods were based mainly on the assumption that figuring out a word was all that was needed. The text was presented in stilted sentences that in no way resembled real speech. From the 1960s through the 1990s, interest in how children learned to read sparked a wave of research (K. Goodman 1968, 1969; F. Smith 1983; B. Cambourne 1988).

Chart 12.2

CHOOSING BOOKS

Parents unfamiliar with children's literature should take advantage of the public libraries and school librarians to obtain information on what is appropriate for their child. Bookstores should be able also to provide guidance on making choices. Libraries and bookstores will sometimes provide an opportunity to meet an author and receive an autographed copy of a book. What a wonderful way to introduce your child to the excitement of meeting a literary figure.

Type of Books	Sample Titles	Possible Focus
Patterned Text & Predictable Books	• Mother Goose Anthologies • Dr. Seuss Books	• Rhyming words • Predicting skills
Concept Books	• The Very Hungry Caterpillar (Eric Carle) • Alphabet Books • Counting Books	• Basic concepts such as counting, alphabet colors & days of the week
Cumulative Tales	• Bringing the Rain to Kepiti Plain (Verna Aardema) • There was an Old Woman Who Swallowed a Fly (traditional tale)	• Listening skills • Memory • Predicting • Picking out details
Picture Books Without Text	• Frog Where Are You? (Mercer Mayer)	• Using clues from pictures • Interpreting a story
Folk Tales and Old Favorites	• Olivia (Ian Falconer) • Mother Goose's Little Treasures, Opie & Wells • Don't let the pigeon drive the bus (Willems) • Grandma, Grandpa, and Me (Mercer Mayer)	• Recalling details • Relating story to personal • Experience • Predicting skills • Vocabulary extension

For all that we have learned about how reading begins, phonics—one of the least effective strategies—continues to attract followers. Perhaps this is because the systematic drill and practice method appeals to our adult need to control the process. In my early teaching, when phonics was the primary way we introduced reading, I found that some children got it easily and others not at all, with no in between. I did not understand in those early days that they lack something we now call *phonemic awareness*. This involves the ability to recognize visual and auditory differences in letters of the alphabet as well as to blend sounds together. For most children the ability to connect sounds with their corresponding letters of the alphabet will be in place by age six, although not necessarily so. Phonemic awareness is not taught directly but comes naturally through play with language, rhymes, and songs. Books such as the Dr. Seuss series that are based on rhyming words are a great way to foster phonemic awareness.

Over my career I've watched methods and approaches go in and out of favor, but one fact that I have found to remain constant is that early reading is most successful when children read about their own immediate experiences.

As a third-year teacher, I had come to realize that two phonics lessons a day in grade one was not the answer. I also had become bored with the repetitive text of the pre-primer readers we used. One day, after returning from a visit to the Vancouver Aquarium, I began to create a story about what the children had seen. Soon we had many pages of chart paper full. To my amazement the next morning the children asked to read these charts. So began my venture into reading materials created for and with the children. I discovered that children who, time and again, confused "something" with "surprise" in the pre-primer were reading words like aquarium and octopus. Combining this with encouraging children to write about events in their own lives is a sure-fire way to get young children into reading and writing.

The importance of using firsthand experiences cannot be overemphasized. Shortly after I began to write these stories, I discovered the work of Sylvia Ashton-Warner (1963). In describing her experiences of teaching Maori children in New Zealand, she wrote that the primary source of beginning reading materials is the children's experiences. Time and again this has been confirmed for me as I watch children thrive when given a combined telling of an event, having it written down, and then reading it back. This is particularly true of the late reader. This is another excellent way for parents to encourage early reading.

When a parent or teacher suspects that a child has a genuine disability with respect to reading, he should consult experts who can help him understand what is going on. It may be something as treatable as needing glasses or it may be a much more serious problem in processing information. In any event a decision to seek intervention must not be based solely on age or even experience. Time may be the single biggest factor in when an individual child starts to read, and we can give no better gift than respecting our child's individual differences. There is no evidence to suggest that anything works better than reading to your child and encouraging a solid foundation of oral language for promoting learning to read.

The focus on reading has shifted away from teaching reading to children learning how to read. The emergence of reading is a marvelous process to watch as it unfolds over the first half dozen or so years of life. Parents and teachers need to use common sense and put reading in perspective along with all of the essential learning that is taking place during this critical period of learning. As Frank Smith (1983) has suggested, however, we ought not to sit back and wait for some magical day for the child to read, but rather we must make sure that her mind is well stocked by her experiences with stories and reading in everyday life.

What Can We Do To Help?

- ➢ Choose good quality literature. There is a reason that certain authors and particular titles remain popular down through generations. Traditional folklore is a rich source of multilayered stories that take the young child off into fantasy while helping adolescent children consider moral issues.

- ➢ From birth, rhymes and jingles delight young children. Many parents instinctively make up nonsense rhymes and words as they play with their baby. Word games and rhymes are an important and enjoyable way to teach children a good deal about language and eventually reading.

> ➢ Children need to play with writing before they can be expected to learn the technical conventions of grammar, punctuation, and spelling. Invented spelling is as important to writing as babbling is to talk.

It is not a cliché to say that reading begins in the home. Long before school, parents play an important role in setting a child on the way. The practice of reading to young children and encouraging them to play with books, catalogues, and other printed material has long been recognized as a significant benefit to children.

For further suggestions see Part 4 Resources: Early Reading Activities.

*I reach my hand into the mind of the child and
the stuff I find there becomes his first reader.*
Sylvia Ashton-Warner

13
Math, Science, Technology, and Play

Science is everywhere around us, from the early morning fog that immobilizes the airport to the burning toast, from the flooded carburetor to the first robin of spring, from your personal home computer to the five pounds you gained on your summer vacation. Whether it's pearls, or butterflies or popcorn, it's science. Whether it's the weather, toxic waste or the moon, it's science. Whether it's gravity or oil spills, it's still science. What can children do to increase their understanding of science? Everything! The options are virtually unlimited.

Selma Wasserman and George Ivany

Young children at play are the true prototypes of the scientist and the mathematician. During play, children constantly probe, question, and explore, take things apart and put them back together, often in unexpected ways. This process of inquiry through play is the way children learn the basics of scientific, mathematical, and technological thinking. We may become exasperated by our child's compulsion to ask why, but this curiosity and thirst to know is the foundation for mathematics and science achievement. Curiosity and wonder at the workings of the world should be celebrated and appreciated as one of childhood's greatest gifts.

When we think about science and mathematics in today's world, we include technology as a product of both. In early learning we do not separate these aspects of thinking into separate "subjects" but see that a young child's exploration and discovery involves all three. The underlying "big ideas," as Selma Wasserman (1990) calls them, are the basis for the investigative experiences that lead to higher levels of thinking. Understanding such big ideas as "machines and tools help us work" and "living things grow and change" comes about through repeated investigation and observation, much of which is derived through play.

Basic Mental Processes

In order to support the development of the mind, it is helpful if we understand the basic mental processes that are at work. These processes develop simultaneously with language and form the foundation for mathematics, science, and technology. These processes are classification and sorting, putting things in order, understanding relationships to space, and number.

Classification and sorting is the way the human brain organizes information about the world. This process begins very early as babies start to distinguish familiar voices and faces. Later boys are separated from girls. To toddlers all animals are dogs (or cats, if they have one as a pet). Gradually, they are able to sort animals into groups according to their personal experiences.

Objects are sorted according to attributes including color, shape, size, and texture, as well as use (things that can cut), locomotion (things that move by themselves), and so on.

Putting things in order is the process of organizing people, things, and events according to a pattern. The pattern, or arranging things by size or shape, shows this process in action. It is this process that leads to ordering events in the day, such as getting up, having breakfast, and so on. It is the basis for our calendar as well as our system for keeping track of time.

Relationships to space refer to understanding about how things are connected in terms of space. How many teaspoons of sugar fit into a cup? How many glasses of juice does the pitcher hold? It also involves how we see ourselves as objects in space. Will this large person fit into that chair? These are very complicated notions for young children. Think for a moment about how difficult it is to have four-year-olds line up one behind the other. Or ask a three-year-old to stand in front of a chair. Spatial relationships also include the relation between objects and space. Watch a two-year-old trying to stuff a large stuffed toy down the toilet. Apart from the dangers of such an exploration, this is the way they figure out the relationship between size and space. These ideas are so automatic to us that we forget how much experience and developmental maturity is needed for a child to grasp the notion of space.

Understanding number means far more than simply counting. It means understanding that four is always four no matter what objects make up the group. The size of the objects doesn't make a difference—four tiny buttons and four huge pumpkins are both four. When they grasp the idea that number only changes when we add something or remove it, children have reached a critical milestone that enables them to proceed with the number operations of addition and subtraction.

Problem solving comes naturally to young children. The trouble is that they don't always find the most efficient or safest solution. Two-year-old Josh knows that the cookies are kept on the top shelf of the kitchen cupboard, so up he climbs, first on a chair and then onto the counter. He still can't reach the cookies, so he stands on a cookbook that's sitting on the counter. By balancing on one foot and standing on tiptoes, he just manages to get hold of the jar. Fortunately, before the whole thing can come crashing down, including Josh, Mom comes into the kitchen. It is very difficult in this situation to stand back and praise Josh's problem-solving skills, but in retrospect his Mom was impressed with his ingenuity.

The foundation for these skills is self-directed play. From infancy through childhood, children perform tasks over and over that enable them to discover and to firmly establish the foundation for math and science thinking. With each new experience the existing pathways in the brain change to allow for new learning.

Technology through Play

In today's world, children are comfortable with technology from an early age. Although we tend to think of computers when we think of technology, it is a form of knowledge that applies understandings and skills of math and science to solve problems using materials, energy, and tools, including computers.

Chart 13.1

PLAY AND TECHNOLOGY	
Remember that there is no right and wrong way to do things. By encouraging children to find solutions we nurture the imagination and strengthen thinking processes. In time, children come to understand that there may be more efficient ways of doing something but valuable lessons occur along the way.	
Elements of Technology	**Play Experiences**
Structures • The physical parts and the ways in which they are constructed	• Many and varied experiences building with blocks, sand, wood, and other materials
Materials • The substance from which the structure is made	• Exploration with cloth, wood, clay, and other materials to discover properties and see how best each can be used
Mechanisms • The parts of the structure that allow it to function	• Experimenting with simple machines (e.g., wheels, gears, hinges, scissors, pliers, etc.) • Pop-up books • Toys with movable parts
Forces • The resource that allows the mechanisms to work	• Experimenting with lever, pulleys, ramps, water guns, and other things that generate motion
Systems • Combinations of structures	• Putting sets of blocks together, creating a toy village in the sandbox, including roads, bridges, etc. • Tools help us work
Functions • The uses to which the structure or system are put	• Exploring form and function Why is the tower bigger at the bottom than the top?

Building the foundations of technology through play is so obvious that we take it for granted. Perhaps block play provides the best illustration of how technology is explored in play. There is a reason why block play holds such fascination for young children, for it is in the playing with blocks that children begin to discover how structures work. They learn about gravity and energy long before they can put language on these notions. They begin to see the connection between form and function. Through practically every play experience, from playing musical instruments to climbing a dome, children experience technology. The following are some suggestions for encouraging technology through play:

- Make a variety of tools available for different play experiences

    o Stapler and scissors for making booklets

    o Egg beater, corkscrew, and thermometer at the home center

    o Ramps and pulleys added to the blocks

- For children who have an interest, set up a mini construction site consisting of a workbench, complete with a vise, hammer, and other woodworking tools. Provide scraps of soft wood and glue. This is one play activity you will want to supervise carefully depending on the maturity and experience of your child.

- Cooking provides valuable experience in the use of simple machines found around the kitchen such as a micro plane for grating citrus rind or a bottle opener.

- Make a collection of wheels (e.g., roller skates, bicycles and tires from various kinds of toys). Encourage your child to use these for play and construction projects.

- Become a junk collector! Save containers of all shapes, sizes, and materials:

    o Small interesting boxes from a make-up counter

- o   Sturdy boxes such as those from a computer store

- o   Shoeboxes and other garment boxes

- o   Sturdy tubes such as those from carpets, as well as smaller ones

- o   Objects that could be used as props for the block play (e.g., wheels, pie plates, etc.)

- Store items in a large, clear plastic bag or storage bin that is easy for your child to access and put things away in.

Block play has long been part of the landscape of childhood. Decades ago letters of the alphabet and numerals were added to sneak in something "useful." Fortunately, few if any children ever pay attention to these features, so intent are they in playing with the blocks. In addition to the benefits to physical development, blocks offer tremendous opportunity for learning the basic foundation of mathematics and science. Although knowledge and skills have been compartmentalized into subject areas, children's learning knows no such artificial limits.

Block play allows us a window into how the child integrates learning through play. As she builds a structure, she is exploring basic science such as gravity and balance; she is exploring mathematical concepts such as spatial relations and Euclidian geometry; she is finding a medium for expressing her creativity; and she may well be practicing her social and language skills if playing in the company of other children.

In the 1930s an early childhood educator named Harriet Johnson began to document what children did with blocks. Her description of the stages of development is a classic study for anyone interested in young children. Along with Caroline Pratt, Harriet Johnson designed the building blocks we've seen for decades in nursery schools and kindergarten classrooms. We owe much of what we know about the value of block play to these pioneer women who recognized and championed children's play.

Adults, who look upon block building as an idle pastime or a childish activity, often fail to realize that block building is a lifetime activity. Whether one is an architect planning a building, a delivery person loading a truck, or a homemaker storing groceries in the cupboard, each is handling various units or forms that fit together in different spatial relations and are influenced by balance and stability. So it is for children as they build with blocks.

Mary Moffitt

For an excellent resource on the work of Harriet Johnson and Carolyn Pratt see *The Block Book, revised edition, edited by* Elizabeth Hirsch (NAEYC).

Types of Blocks

Hollow Wooden Blocks

Considered standard equipment in preschool and kindergarten classrooms, these large blocks are best suited to ages three and up.

Unit Blocks

First designed by Caroline Pratt, founder of what is now called the Banks Street School in New York City, these plain blocks are recognized for their value in developing mathematics and science concepts and are usually found in preschools and kindergartens.

Sets of these blocks vary in type and accessories depending upon the manufacturer. All unit blocks, however, are based on a ratio of 1:2:4 or half as high as they are wide and twice as long as they are wide. This allows for many combinations in building. In addition to the proportioned blocks, there are also cylinders and curved pieces that conform in height, width, and thickness to the unit blocks. Some sets have additional accessories to encourage a broad range of structures. It is important that there be sufficient numbers of each type of block to allow for ambitious building.

Table Blocks and Geometric Shapes

There are a wide variety of small blocks and three-dimensional shapes to complement the larger unit and hollow blocks. These may vary in size to accommodate the developmental needs of young children.

Samples of additional table blocks and shapes

- Attribute blocks

- Pattern blocks

- Interlocking cubes

- Freestanding cubes

As children move through the stages in block play, they are discovering principles of structure and force and are learning some important understandings related to the *properties of blocks*:

- Three-dimensional blocks have the properties of shape and size as well as measurement of height, length, and weight.

- Similarities and differences in curves and angles can be observed.

- Corners, edges, and faces can be explored.

- Blocks can be placed in different positions (e.g., on end, on their side, or laid flat).

Children also learn the difficult notion of a *block structure as an interrelated system*. This means that they explore how each individual piece relates to the whole project. If one piece is out of joint with the others, the structure cannot work. For example, when building a bridge, both support pieces must be the same length and at the right distance apart to support the crosspiece. Children also come to understand ratios as they struggle to improvise when a particular length block is needed but they have all been used. They will discover that two smaller blocks equal the length of the larger one and so continue with the construction.

Through repeated block play, a child comes to understand that there are particular sequential patterns that can be followed in creating a system. The child develops a number of these systems or patterns of action that make construction efficient and successful. This is perhaps best illustrated by watching toddlers build a tower. Moving from a random pile, children gradually learn that they must make a graduated tower with a base sufficiently broad to support the tower.

There are many other things that children learn through block play related to language and working together. When the block play is spontaneously undertaken, it leads to themes of the children's making. The children are more invested in themes of their own choosing than those initiated by the teacher.

In his study *How Constructive Block Play Supports the Development of Literacy in Kindergarten*, E. R. Tremblay (1998) illustrates the connection between literacy and block play.

The block centre regulars had been building castles from the large wooden blocks for several days so I asked them if they would like to go to the library to get books about castles. Four of the children were quite eager and returned to the classroom with ten books related to castles. After two play periods of working with these books, I left chart paper and markers out near the blocks. This time instead of going directly to building with the blocks, Susan suggested drawing plans for their castles. They drew a series of pictures showing different parts of the castle. Fifteen minutes later, I noticed that Susan and David were directing the others in building according to their plans.

The children put on costumes and as they built they talked in role. During this session, the children had to negotiate with several others who were using some of the big blocks for a different purpose. They used the library books as their resources and they spoke in role about what was going on in the castle. All of this was the spontaneous outcome of the suggestion to go to the library.

Another way of nurturing science, mathematics, and technology is through sand and water play. No one has to show young children how to play with sand or water. They are drawn to these materials as surely as they are drawn to food and affection. Play with both of these materials offers countless opportunities to learn the big ideas of math and science.

A sandbox is a cherished part of child's play. Whether it is a pristine stretch of beach or a small patch of sand in a vacant lot, children gravitate toward this material. It is a resource for endless building and exploratory play. Along with the natural satisfaction it provides, there are many ideas related to math and science that have their foundation in play with sand and other dry materials.

Chart 13.2

Ideas for Block Play
Suggest blocks as gifts for your child. A collection of interlocking blocks can grow with your children and be a rich source of play into the teen years.
Being a Mechanic • Take boxes of various sizes outdoors • Provide glue, paint, and duct tape • Invite children to create their own vehicles.
Add the following things to block play: • Toy cars, trucks, and other vehicles • Planks or other items that can be used as ramps • Squeeze bottles that could represent oil cans and other types of car-related substances • Mechanics tools
Extend block play • Change the blocks from time to time • Add props and costumes such as a fireman's hat and lengths of hose • Be a play partner helping your child to add language to the experience

Through play with sand and other dry materials children learn the properties of matter:

- Sand has weight and texture.

- Sand can absorb liquids.

- Sand holds its shape when set.

- Sand takes up space and takes the shape of a hollow container.

It is not necessary to have fancy equipment for this kind of play because there are so many opportunities in daily life to play with sand and water. A few inexpensive toys and found materials along with a container that will hold water or sand are all you need.

Water play is universal across cultures and ages. From the silky feel of water as we gently sway back and forth to the awesome sight of the force of water during a raging line squall, water holds fascination for us. Babies love nothing more than splashing about in water. Grownups canoeing across a northern lake at dawn are renewed by the tranquility that water provides. It is no wonder that children love to play in the water.

Through water play children learn the properties of liquids:

- Water has three states—liquid, solid, and steam.

- Water can change from one form to another.

- Water has weight and volume.

- Water goes through some substances but not others.

Children also learn about

- buoyancy,

- evaporation,

- condensation, and

- freezing and melting

Children learn that

- some things dissolve in water, and others do not;

- some things float, while others sink.

Water play can provide the opportunity to begin to teach children about the environmental concerns regarding water, including conserving water and pollution. For older children, focus on a specific idea and provide materials that will lead to understanding of the "big idea."

No one has to teach children how to play with sand or water.

Things to Remember

- Change the water daily.

- Provide aprons and/or waterproof protection. A simple solution is to staple straps onto a piece of oilcloth or heavy-gauge plastic.

- End of summer sales provide an excellent time to stock up on sand and water toys. Keep in mind that, like all toys, it helps to be selective in what you put out at any one time. Throwing too much at children all at once leads to random exploration of the materials and toys. Consider what a child might learn by playing with a particular set of toys and keep the others for another day.

What Can We Do To Help?

> Provide a selection of different types of blocks, both freestanding and interlocking. Add props from time to time that spark new interest and new themes.

Chart 13.3

\	IDEAS FOR SAND AND WATER PLAY		
Sand has volume	**Absorption**	**Buoyancy**	**Liquid to Solid**
• Provide an assortment of containers of different shapes that hold an equal amount. • Let children experiment with filling the containers with sand to observe that a tall thin container may hold the same amount as a wide, shorter one.	• Set out several containers of water • Provide a variety of materials with a range of absorbency (e.g., cotton, wool, leather, oil cloth, paper towel, newspaper, tissue paper, tin foil, plastic wrap, etc.) • Encourage your child to experiment to find which material absorbs the most water, which absorbs the fastest, etc.	• Provide materials for building a boat. Try using egg cartons, aluminum foil, blocks of wood, plasticene, play dough, paper, straws, styrofoam containers, or other comparable material • Have children make boats from the materials to see which will float and observe other things that affect the ability to float (e.g., how many wooden cubes will each hold before sinking?)	• Put water into containers varying in shape & size. Each is about ¾ filled. Add food coloring to containers Place outdoors on a freezing cold afternoon or in a freezer. • The next day, run them under hot water tap to loosen and drop the ice blocks into an empty bin. • Allow for free exploration with this new material. Place blocks back into containers (an excellent spatial task) and refreeze. • After a few days, add sawdust, flour, water, or salt and watch what happens.

> Natural materials attract children, and we need do little else than make sure they have access to water and sand and ice. Check your local library and bookstore for idea books that will have experiments and games to play.

> Encourage children to describe what they are doing and pose questions such as these:

What would happen if you mixed this cooking oil in the water? Let's find out.

How can we get this wall of sand to stay put? (Try wetting it, propping it up with wood, and so on)

Perhaps one of the best science labs is the kitchen. Cooking provides countless opportunities to use mathematics and to observe scientific phenomenon such as dissolving, that water can be liquid, solid or vapor, and so on. Kitchen scales and measuring cups and spoons help children begin to understand quantity and observe relationships between one measure and another. As the opening quote to this chapter suggests, science is indeed all around us.

For further suggestions see Part 4 Resources: Games and Activities for Math

14
Awakening the Artist in the Child

Given the importance of play – not to speak of art – in the cognitive development of children, it seems odd that scholars should neglect what virtually everyone else regards as one of the characteristic features of childhood. If children do anything, they play.

Elliot Eisner

Long before words are used, the arts are the voice of the young child's inner life. Movement and production of primitive artifacts convey joy, sorrow, and fear. Children show the process of discovery in the marks and imprints on the materials they use. Natural materials such as water, wood, and sand are used to express imagination and to lend a quality of permanence to experience.

Producing art requires a child to evoke an experience, idea, or feeling and to find symbols to express it. In this way, the arts are a language that cuts across cultural and social barriers. The arts enable a child to begin to understand his own abilities and perspective as well as opening the way to understanding others. As children come to appreciate how different are the ways others view the world and express their perceptions, they begin to grow in tolerance and acceptance of those who are different.

Art and play have much in common. Both art and play are means of personal expression. Both involve imagination and the use of representational thinking. Both art and play result in a creation. In the case of art, the creation is permanent and can be examined and displayed. In play, the product is fleeting as, for example, an episode of sociodramatic play. Unless captured on film, these magical creations are lost forever.

Art and play are both governed by implicit rules that come naturally to children. They just seem to know what to do. In play, the rules are tied to the form of play, as we see in sociodramatic play. Children who are silly, don't stay in role, or who behave inconsistently with their role will be put out of the play episode. In art, rules such as those that relate to balance and form are intuitively demonstrated long before a child could talk about these elements.

Perhaps the most enduring similarity between art and play is that both are uninhibited and spontaneous. As children reach the middle years there is a natural self-consciousness that hinders self-expression, but with younger children, it is only when adults become critical of what they produce, drawing attention to what the adult sees as "shortcomings," that the natural spontaneity is lost.

Play is a prerequisite for art. Observing young children, we see that they are essentially creative and, at heart, artists. Through early exploration a young child discovers the properties of primitive materials and how to use these to express inner ideas. Children have a natural instinct to make a mark as a unique imprint of themselves. They delight in playing with natural materials such as wood, water, clay, and mud.

Each area of the arts—music, dance, visual art, and drama—appears in the play of young children. Even before birth, the baby responds to music and to the rhythmic movements of dance. These primitive responses carry over into the first months of life when the baby likes nothing more than to be rocked and soothed by a lullaby. Visual stimulation has long been considered a must for the newborn baby. Mobiles that reflect light, make gentle noises, and sway are found in the baby's room from the outset. Even pretend play starts early, as parents playfully put on silly faces and new voices.

As a baby matures into a toddler, art is seen everywhere in play. A toddler mucks about with paint and mud and even her food to create visual art. A three-year-old twirls and skips and bounces through the mall with all the grace of a true ballerina. When digging and squeezing and packing wet sand together, a sandcastle is born out of the chaos of a beach. The six-year-old sculptor is creating an artistic expression that is unique to him. When given the opportunities to explore with different kinds of material, the artist within the child comes alive.

I Hear Music

Music is considered to be the most formal of the arts, but in the early years the essential similarities between play and music remain. We scarcely can think of play without the presence of music. Children spontaneously and unselfconsciously sing and dance their way through play with joy and enthusiasm. They bang and clap and jump to the rhythm of music. As with all aspects of development, some children will have a greater aptitude than others for music and dance. There are, however, some general patterns that most children display.

Whirling Physical Response

From birth to around age five, response to music tends to be spontaneous and free. The following are some milestones on the way to controlled responses to music.

- During the first year, an infant is alert to music and rhythmic movement.

- As early as eight months, he is likely to make musical babbling sounds.

- By age two, a toddler can respond with his whole body as he rocks, marches, and dances to music. A child may begin to move on request but finds it difficult to stop. He can clap quickly but not slowly. His free play with instruments is random and exuberant.

- By age five, he moves with grace. He can clap to a simple rhythm and do the motions of an action song. He still uses instruments as an extension of his own body. This can make it to difficult for most children to actually play an instrument as required.

Controlled Response

- By age three children can respond to and sing familiar chants, rhymes, and songs. They will already have favorites to which they will respond with their whole body as they clap, dance, and march.

- It is quite common at this stage for a young child to change the words to a familiar song.

- Children at this age enjoy songs with repetition such as *There Was an Old Lady Who Swallowed a Fly* or *This Old Man*. Physical movement is still quite awkward and uncontrolled.

- By age five a child who has been exposed to music and singing will likely be able to find his singing voice.

- At this age, he begins to know the difference between high and low, soft and loud.

- Given sufficient opportunity, he can sing in tune and he can now move according to direction, for example, creep like a mouse, gallop like a horse, and so on.

> For suggestions see Resources and References: Handmade Musical Instruments

The Messy Artist

Visual art involves the child in picture making, sculpting, and printmaking. The earliest form of visual art is building three-dimensional figures. As children explore the various media used in visual art, they intuitively begin to develop an understanding of the elements of design—color, form, line, shape, space, texture, and value. These, of course, are not taught, but through play begin to emerge over the first six years of life.

For suggestions see Part 4 Resources: Recipes for Play Dough.

Scribble of Materials

There are distinct patterns in each of the visual arts that help guide parents and teachers to understand a child's development. Up to about fifteen months, the baby will squish play dough, scrunch up paper, and finger paint with whatever is at hand. He also explores the properties of three-dimensional objects. Which blocks can roll and which cannot? Which blocks can stand alone and which need support? At this stage, the experience is tactile not visual, that is, the child goes by feel rather than sight.

At around fifteen months, the toddler begins to arrange materials in a pile, or what I call a *scribble of material*. This action is random and is to no apparent purpose. In other words, he is not building a tower or a bridge. He is simply building. At this stage he is exploring the properties of material as well as the use of space without regard for a finished product. This will come later.

Every parent is aware of the onset of picture making at around eighteen months as the toddler grabs a marker or crayon and scribbles on every available surface. What is frequently looked upon as a nuisance is in fact a stunning achievement. These prerepresentational drawings, which appear to be sheer random motor activities, herald the beginning of artistic expression.

By age two and one half, the scribbles have become purposeful and deliberate, although representational only by accident. At this stage, the child makes the drawing and then decides what it is.

By age three, the messy scribbles give way to experimenting with an array of geometric shapes, including the mandala. The mandala, a cross ensconced in a circle or square, is an ancient symbol found in all cultures. Research has shown that in addition to the mandala, there are twenty different patterns of scribbles as well as seventeen patterns of placement. These early expressions are not trivial but in fact quite complex.

Beginning of Representational Expression

Between the ages of three and four, children generally begin to create three-dimensional structures that represent objects in their world. Over time, these structures become more ambitious in terms of the variety of materials used. Distinct forms and patterns appear as the child begins to decorate and embellish his creations. At this stage, the child shows increased inventiveness in design and a growing awareness of balance and form. There is a deliberate quality now. The child sets out knowing what he intends to make.

Sometime during the third and fourth years, the child produces the first figure that can be called a "person." The first human figures are referred to as tadpoles. A tadpole consists of a circle with marks believed to represent facial features. This tadpole usually has several lines radiating out as appendages. Over time, the child evolves a variety of patterns for familiar objects, such as the house with a chimney, a flower, the sun, and so on, eventually arranging these into a simple scene. Throughout this stage, children begin to develop solutions for graphic challenges such as using a ladder to represent a staircase.

> *Rhoda Kellogg was one of the first to study the development of visual art in young children. Her description has become a classic. It can be found accompanied by an insightful discussion in the book* The Arts and Human Development *by Howard Gardner.*

The decline of creativity in artistic expression can also be traced in large measure to the inappropriate but strongly rooted practices of crafts in the early years. In preschool and kindergarten, there is a long-standing tradition of teacher-directed crafts that serve to teach children from the earliest age to follow rigid ideas and a prescribed approach to art. This is where the notion of only one right way to do something begins. It is also the beginnings of the focus on the end product rather than the process of self-expression.

I was in a junior kindergarten classroom observing a teacher candidate. She had been assigned a lesson in making a drum as a Christmas tree ornament. I was impressed with the thoroughness of her preparation. She had purchased small Styrofoam cylinders and prepared strips of cloth cut to fit exactly around a cylinder. She had glue for sticking and sparkly decorations to add. She also had a model to show what it should look like.

The teacher candidate began by asking for five volunteers to come to the craft table. Five eager ones joined her, and following the directions as she showed them how, they completed quite respectable-looking drums. These were the children with excellent eye-hand coordination who also knew how to follow directions quite well. They also showed an interest in the craft, and as one child said to me, "My mom's going to love this!"

When finished, of course all at the same time, the teacher candidate asked for another group. Four came willingly and the fifth came to join a friend. With a little more help following directions, this group, too, moved along in an orderly fashion. The third group was a little more difficult to persuade, but they too completed the required craft but without the enthusiasm. Their drums didn't sport the dazzling designs of the first two groups. Clearly, they were working as quickly as possible in order to get back to play.

It was with the final group that things got really difficult. They simply ignored the request to come to the table and continued on at the playhouse center busily absorbed in their play. The teacher candidate knew that this would not be acceptable to the host teacher, and she looked to me for guidance. Before the candidate had a chance to make a decision, the host teacher marched over and drew the four remaining children over to the table, accompanied by a scolding about being uncooperative.

I asked the candidate during our debriefing what she had learned from this experience. "Well, for one thing," she replied, "I think as far as those last few children were concerned, they could care less about making a drum. They would have been happier if I had just left them alone."

She recognized that there were some benefits to children learning how to follow directions and master the use of small tools. She also realized that for most of these children, this task was busywork that took them away from what they really were interested in doing, that is, play.

In terms of what she might have done had the host teacher not interfered, she suggested that she would leave the materials and try later on. She did not think it would be appropriate to let them get away without doing an assigned task. When I asked her why this was so, she couldn't come up with a strong rationale why all of these children needed to make the same ornament at the same time and in the same way.

In her placement the next term, when assigned another craft activity (a favorite assignment for candidates in a kindergarten placement), she gathered a variety of containers with lids from which the children would make musical instruments. She had bins with different types of noisemakers (e.g., beans, pebbles, and rice), and different kinds of paper (e.g., tissue and crepe paper, as well as scraps of cloth with various materials for trim). She did not produce a finished model, but she demonstrated different sounds using the different kinds of containers—some were made of plastic, some tin, others glass.

She did not have to coax children to the craft table. Seven children came immediately, and they played for some time, experimenting with the different combinations. The teacher candidate then asked them to make a choice and create their instrument. These seven were still working on their creations as others joined. Some watched; others got right into exploring the materials. This center remained a hive of activity for the whole morning. Not all children ended up with an instrument, but without exception all children explored the materials. The finished products were then placed in a special tote box and added to the classroom collection of instruments.

It goes without saying that bringing exploratory play into the process greatly enriched the experience. I noticed on a later visit that the shakers became props for play as well as musical instruments to accompany their singing and dancing. The techniques that they used to make the shakers were used in making other props for their sociodramatic play.

Coloring Books, Stencils, and Crafts

In homes and preschools for generations, coloring books, stencils, and adult-directed crafts have been a mainstay. These activities are often calming and are useful as quiet activities when necessary. They also provide the opportunity to develop fine muscle control and perhaps learn how to use basic tools such as scissors and glue. These are not, however, visual art. In fact, too much of this kind of limiting activity will soon inhibit the child and erode self-expression. Children get the message that their primitive attempts are not up to standard and begin to rely on prepared material instead of producing art of their own. Not only do these activities inhibit growth in creative expression, but they also erode the child's sense of accomplishment. There are many more productive activities to provide without wasting the child's time on such endeavors.

Pretend Play: A Kaleidoscope of Creativity

As described in chapter 3, pretend play is a rich activity that develops imagination, representational thinking, language, social development, and a host of other benefits. It begins in the simple personal imitative behavior of the toddler and develops into the amazing imaginative activity that we call sociodramatic play.

The Awaking of Imagination

All children indulge in pretend play. Imagination appears around age two when the toddler pretends to feed his dolly or take him for a walk in the stroller. Initially, there is a fine line between imagination and imitation. Toddlers imitate the everyday actions they see. Gradually, imitation gives way to imagination as they take what they see and make new actions. Imaginary creatures appear, and eventually, imaginary friends. The onset of pretend play coincides with the rapid development of language between ages two and three.

A few simple items of clothing, in particular shoes and hats, will spark a child's imagination. When items are first put out for play, little ones are likely to try everything on before settling into a role.

Sociodramatic play will develop and grow over the years between ages four and seven. In sociodramatic play, children go beyond imitation to re-creations of experience. Imitation appears to be the entry behavior for dramatic play, while imagination enables this power to soar.

When I first began to study sociodramatic play, I thought of it as a mosaic of pieces each related but individual. As I got deeper and deeper into the world of children's sociodramatic play, I came to describe it not as a mosaic but a flutter of butterflies. Just when you think you know who is who and where the play is going, the players take flight in a different direction.

In order to understand what is happening and what learning is taking place, I found it helpful to think of sociodramatic play as having four elements—theme, roles, action plan, and language. By understanding how each of these elements works, we can better appreciate the complexity and wonder of this form of make-believe.

The themes of sociodramatic play fall into three groups—family, community, and episodes based on media characters from books, movies, or television. The theme and actions always reflect the immediate culture of the children.

The simplicity of sociodramatic play may lead adults to believe it is trivial, but there are some who would argue that children's play is a search for meaning in human experience (Courtney 1982; Weininger 1982). One of the most persistent themes in folklore and myth that emerges in children's sociodramatic play is the powerlessness of the child. Time and again we see the child delivered helpless into the power of terrible enemies, but the child inevitably conquers the evil forces. The world is seen as a stage on which forces struggle for control of the child.

The death and rebirth metaphor is another that is consistently found in sociodramatic play. This ancient and profound theme is generally intertwined with the use of magic, as illustrated in the following episode of the Reindeer Adventures.

Three children climb into a rocking boat, now a sleigh, and pretend to go for a ride. Suddenly, they pull over and "stop the engine."

Margrit: "There's a wild cat out there."

Franco: "Santa, there's a wild cat there."

Ernie: "There's more than just two."

Franco: "All right. Rudolph, you stay inside. Okay?"

Margrit: "Okay, guys. Let's go!"

The children jump out of the sleigh and chase the imaginary wild cats. They make gestures with their arms and bark noisily. Franco falls over.

Ernie: "Oh my God. One of the reindeers is dead!"

Margrit: "No, he's just pretending. I'll get my magic."

Margrit waves her arms in circular motions over Franco, and he jumps to his feet.

Ernie: "Hey. Let's get back in the sleigh. We can play again."

The *action plan* for sociodramatic play is a framework of common everyday actions. The most common actions are eating, going to bed, nurturing the baby, shopping, riding a bus, and having a party. In any one episode the same actions may be repeated over and over as seen in the anecdotes above.

The rhythm of an action plan is punctuated by digressions. Sometimes an individual moves off into a different theme. Sometimes the whole group shifts as seen when three of the four players in an episode of hospital decide to go shopping and leave the patient alone. After a brief digression, the three return and resume the hospital theme.

The *roles* in sociodramatic play do not represent a cast of characters but rather a set of relationships—nurturer and child, caregiver and patient, shopkeeper and shopper, bus driver and rider. When playing hospital, for example, there may be several caregivers, but they are not differentiated into doctors, nurses, and assistants. Rather, they tend to the patient, performing the rituals children know about, such as giving a needle and taking a temperature.

Children tend to assume adult roles over those of children, and the themes and action plans explore adult life. Being assigned the role of the child is reserved for the less mature child. Even an adult is usually assigned a lesser role. It is, after all, the children's world not ours. The richer the child's experiences with human relationships, the greater the store of roles from which to draw. We may not always be comfortable with the roles they assume, but we must remember that they are trying to make sense of the world as they know it.

In early sociodramatic play, children tend to play in pairs. Several pairs of children may be playing together, but each pair is developing its own action plan. In time, other children will be encouraged to join in, and pairs will come together to form quite complex actions. The most elaborate episodes, that is, ones requiring a high level of language and social development as well as imagination, will always have a mature player to provide leadership and keep the play on track. Less skillful players are not likely to be able to sustain a complicated episode and will revert to playing in pairs. This pattern goes on well past kindergarten.

An episode based on the familiar story of *Rudolph the Red-Nosed Reindeer* illustrates how children rework what they know and understand of the world into pretend play. While all of the children know the story, they cannot imagine a world in which travel is not done by way of motorized vehicles. Thus, the reindeer do some surprising actions.

It is nearing Christmas, and the classic favorite Rudolph the Red-Nosed Reindeer has just been aired on television. James and Marcus join with several friends to play Rudolph. All of the reindeer are herded together under a display table that has become the reindeers' home. They bring bowls for food, books to read, and pillows.

Marcus, directing the others announces, "Time for bed."

The reindeer neigh and kick up their feet in imitation of animal behavior.

Then the players curl up under the table as if sleeping.

After several seconds, Marcus calls, "Ding, ding, morning."

They all get up, jump into the rocking boat that has become a sleigh.

"Vroom, vroom," says Marcus as he turns the key to start the sleigh, and off they drive to deliver toys.

This episode went for over one-half hour with the players repeating the going to bed, getting up, and driving off a number of times.

This delightful episode shows how the children interpret a story through their own experiences. In their world, if you are going someplace, you drive. The reindeer have somehow become Santa's helpers. It is interesting, however, that they bring a flavor of reality by having the reindeer speak in neighing-like sounds, kicking their heels up in imitation of an animal, and even eating from their bowls without using their hands.

In order for an episode of sociodramatic play to work, children must have sufficient language to talk about what they want to do and to carry on a conversation that sounds like the real situation. The change into character requires a signal. It may be that the child adopts a particular pose consistent with the new role or changes her voice to reflect the role.

Clara, Jemi, and Migual are playing in the home center. Marco puts on a tool belt from the dress-up box, walks over to the home center, and shouts, "Lady. Oh, Lady. Is this the place where the furnace is busted?"

Clara without any prompting answers, "Ya. Come on in."

"What's wrong with it?" asks Marco.

"How should I know?" answers Clara with hand on hip.

The signal for the transformation into the repairperson was twofold. Marco signaled his intent to become the repairperson by putting on the tool belt, and then when he spoke, it was in a tone and inflection of an adult. There was no need for him to explicitly suggest that they might play repairperson.

Marco's mother, who happened to be visiting that day, told me that they had indeed had furnace trouble several days earlier. While this was not an exact re-creation, it had an authenticity that was remarkable. The way the children spoke, their gestures and intonation all were quite different from how they talked and acted during an episode of family. They captured the nuances of the service person to a tee.

Throughout an episode, children must move in and out of these two functions of talk. When a player does not stay in character or perhaps takes off on another theme, the leader is likely to drop out of character and try to get things back on track. When all else fails, we hear the familiar phrase, "Then you can't play!"

This form of play is seen to be an essential ingredient for healthy development and the learning needed for school success. In sociodramatic play, a child moves from mere imitation to re-creation of experience, and is provided with opportunities to explore new realities.

Drama

By age eight, sociodramatic play begins to give way to drama. Children who have actively engaged in sociodramatic play will find drama an effective way to communicate. Drama will become a powerful means of communication in the middle years.

What Can We Do To Help?

> ➢ Take the arts seriously and encourage your child to express herself through the arts. At each new stage provide appropriate materials and tools—crayons, play dough, clay, cloth, various kinds of paper, tin foil and other media as well as scissors, paint brushes, and so on. Working in wood is very satisfying, provided that the child can manipulate it. Very hard wood is frustrating, but chunks of Styrofoam and soft wood are manageable. Children can use certain types of glue to hold these materials together, and in time, can learn to use a hammer and nails. A workbench fitted with a vise is an excellent addition to your child's play area.

Chart 14.1

SUPPORTING EMERGING ARTISTS
• A child should be surrounded with all kinds of music (e.g., traditional children's songs, classical, pop, and music from other cultures). • Sing with your child often. If you do not have a great voice, no matter! Young children just want to sing with you. • Sing songs you enjoy yourself. It does not much matter what you sing as that you sing. Your favorite ballad or rock and roll hit will work equally well to stimulate musical response. • Quality recordings make a wonderful gift for a child. These provide countless hours of enjoyment. • Provide a collection of rhythm instruments, both commercial and homemade. • Where possible take your child to hear a live performance. Many libraries and community centers provide this kind of entertainment, particularly at holiday times. Think of this as a possible way to entertain for a birthday party.
• Assume a positive attitude toward the child's early art, recognizing that each step is important and necessary for the development of self-expression. • Don't be afraid of mess. Finger painting is a wonderful sensory experience enjoyed by children of all ages.
• Children do not need a lot of expensive toys and materials to spark imaginative play. • Make materials available that can be used to create props (e.g., pieces of cloth, tissue paper, newspaper, assorted boxes and containers, sequins, beads, buttons, ribbon, string etc.). Have the necessary tools available as well (e.g., scissors, glue, pins, stapler, tape etc.). • Try putting together a prop box with items from around the house. • Add markers, pencils/pens, and paper to encourage writing through making lists, taking orders, and making greeting cards. • Add catalogues, magazines, and storybooks to encourage reading. • When invited, join in the pretend play in-role. Let children lead you!

> ➤ When not sure what the child has made, ask her to tell you about the picture or creation. Learn what to look for as signs of the development of symbolism in art so that you can recognize significant milestones when they occur.

> ➤ Children learn to sing and dance by singing and dancing. The child needs to be surrounded with all kinds of music, and

be sure to share your personal favorites with her. Recognize spontaneous dramatic play as the richest form of play, and encourage it by joining in.

> For further suggestions see Part 4 Resources: Putting Together a Dress-up Box.

The arts contribute much more than relaxation and fun. Each of the arts can be linked to academic achievement as well as the development of self-expression. For some children it will be the beginning of a life as an artist. Whether amateur or professional, the rewards are immeasurable.

15

Returning Play to Our Children

Children cannot speak for themselves. They rely on us to protect their rights. In terms of education this means recognizing play as the premier way children learn. As presented throughout this book, we have sound reason to believe in the power of play to give every child the best beginning possible for healthy growth and development. Without play it is likely that children will be robbed of some important aspects of development that can never be recovered.

Better Beginnings

In speaking out for young children, we add our voices to a growing number of experts who see the first years as crucial to leading a productive life. Experts from the fields of medicine, biology, and economy have joined educators, sociologists, and psychologists in expressing concern about the consequences to society of not providing our children with a good start in life. This is not new. We've known for a long time how important the early years are to personal growth and development. We've known that many serious problems in adulthood have their beginnings in the early years. What has changed is the focus of the arguments. Today, the discussion is around two key areas. The first relates to new discoveries about human development, in particular that of the brain. The second relates to the issue of human capital, that is, the economic importance of providing our children with the best possible start in life.

Fraser Mustard, a medical doctor and internationally recognized expert in early childhood development, is among those who have led the call for better beginnings for children based on the understandings of how the brain develops and the long-term effects of early intervention.

Mustard concludes that experienced-based brain development in the early years of life sets the neurological and biological pathways that affect health and well-being throughout life. He argues that in order to make a difference to the way in which children grow, we need to look at how the brain develops in the dynamic period of brain development from birth through age five. In an address to the Canadian Education Association, *What Do We Know about Early Learning and What Are We Doing about It?* he said, "Most of you in education are plugging into it [intervention] later on in child development. Some trajectories in learning and behavior may already be set by the time children enter the school system" (Mustard 2005).

The biological pathways that form through sensory exploration during the early years last a lifetime. The early biological changes in the brain affect both the physical and the mental health of adults, as well as their capacity to learn and their behavior. A compelling argument for supporting early development is that, as Richard Tremblay of CIFAR suggests (Tremblay, Haapasalo, and Masse 1994; Masse and Tremblay 1997), a child's behavior and the capacity to learn may already be set by the time she enters school. As Tremblay's studies show, serious problems do not go away with intervention in schools. The solution lies in preventing these problems during the first critical years of life.

> *For additional information on experience-based brain and biological development see the web site for Canadian Institute for Advanced Research, Dr. Ronald Barr, Director, University of British Columbia, Canada.*

More recently, concern for the quality of development and care of our youngest citizens has become an economic issue. There is significant evidence that money spent in quality care and education for young children is a solid, long-term investment. A growing number of economists have begun to advocate for investment in the early years. There is general agreement that good beginnings for children pay high returns for the economy later on. Since releasing its groundbreaking report *Preschool for All: Investing in a Productive and Just Society,* the Committee for Economic Development in the United States, an independent, non-partisan organization, has engaged in an aggressive national campaign to build momentum for investment in early education. This momentum was given a significant boost at their 2007 conference, *Building the Economic Case for Investment in Children.* This work is continuing through such initiatives as Investing in kids Working Group and The Science of Learning, Behavior, and Health: Closing the Gap between What We Know and What We Do, a colloquium Series sponsored by the Center on the Developing Child at Harvard University (2007-2008).

> For further information on these and other related issues see:
> http://www.ced.org.

Among the economists who have spoken out passionately on this issue is Dr. James Heckman, a Nobel Prize winner in economics. His research into problems of economic growth in the United States led him to conclude that human capital is the key to economic growth. In a presentation to the Canadian Education Association (2005), Fraser Mustard quotes Heckman as saying, "We cannot afford to postpone investing in children until they become adults nor can we wait until they are school age - a time when it may be too late to intervene" In an interview published online by Children of the Code Series (2007), Heckman argues that, while intervention may work later, the effectiveness is far less and the costs far greater than investing in developing a solid foundation for learning in the early years.

So What is Being Done?

The United States has a long tradition of concern for the early years, and in particular, as this relates to disadvantaged children. From

Operation Head Start in the late 1960s through today, a number of projects have been aimed at improving the early years for children and families. Through initiatives such as No Child Left Behind and Good Start, Grow Smart, the United States has continued to try to find ways of improving the quality of care and education for its children. No Child Left Behind was undertaken with great promise when President George Bush enacted it into law in 2001.

While the intent of this bill is laudable, major concerns have surfaced regarding how quality is to be achieved. The main focus seems to be on standards-based educational reform with an emphasis on measurable results. Some leading American experts believe that this places the initiative in jeopardy from the beginning.

> *For information on childcare in the United States see National Child Care Information Center, U. S. Department of Health and Human Services.*

In Canada, similar initiatives have been undertaken. The federal government has made a number of promises over the past decade, but to date little has been done to create long-term solutions to improving childcare and early education. *The British Columbia Early Childhood Development Action Plan: A Work in Progress* is an initiative that sets out a wide range of actions to improve services for children and their families in that province. In Ontario, a major study was undertaken to assess the childcare issue. The *Early Years Study: Final Report* (McCain and Mustard 1999) presented a series of recommendations aimed at prevention and intervention in the early years. These include the following:

- early child development and parenting centers

- community networks linking public health, schools, and social services

- a consolidated government ministry that encompasses all of the existing branches of government that affect children and families

While money has been allocated for services, for creating childcare spaces, and for addressing some of the concerns about the need to consolidate the various governmental agencies responsible for care and education, progress is painfully slow.

> *For current information on childcare in Canada see Friendly, Martha, Jane Beach, Carolyn Ferns and Michele Turiano. Early Childhood Education and Care in Canada 2006. Published by Childcare Canada, Childcare Resource and Research Unit (CRRU) Toronto, On.*

Several projects in Australia outline action plans for improvement to early development. The Best Start initiative developed by the state government of Victoria in Australia (Government of Victoria, Australia, Department of Human Services and Education 2007), is dedicated to providing the best possible environment, experiences, and care for young children from pregnancy to school. It has a strong emphasis on prevention and intervention. Good Beginnings is a national initiative funded by the Australian government and various philanthropic charities. It describes a wide range of early intervention programs aimed at improving children's start in life.

Between 1998 and 2000, ten countries, including Sweden, Belgium, Denmark, and the United Kingdom, participated along with Canada and the United States in a project under the auspices of the Organization for Economic Cooperation and Development (OECD). Since then, ten additional countries have joined the project. The project, titled Thematic Review of Early Childhood Education and Care (1999), was designed to improve policy-making in early care and education. The Scandinavian countries have been much further ahead in terms of the recognition for support to families during the early years. This project strengthened the initiatives in many of the participating countries.

> For information regarding the progress being made in the twenty participating countries of the Organization for Economic Cooperation and Development, see Starting Strong II: Early Childhood Education and Care (OECD, 2006).

There are some positive signs that awareness of the value of quality experiences for young children is genuine. New policies are being introduced such as the one recently enacted in the province of Ontario to provide full-day junior and senior kindergarten for all children in the province as a start to offering a seamless day for children. In the case of early childhood development and learning, an investment of serious money is more than welcome. Money alone, however, is not the answer. Providing a full-day program for four-year-olds, for example, has much merit, but not if what is provided is simply a watered-down first-grade curriculum.

What constitutes a high quality program remains unclear. In the report on the Good Beginnings Australia, it is pointed out that while there are a large number of indicators of the importance of this period (preschool), ranging from brain development to educational outcomes, relatively little work has been done to define what would constitute a positive beginning. What we do know is that a good beginning is a matter of both nature and nurture. It is generally recognized that development and learning is a matter of both genetics and environment. We have tended to believe that in terms of genetics we get what we get, although this may not be entirely true. As noted in a Good Beginnings Australia report,

> "Much of our thinking about the brain has been dominated by old assumptions—that the genes we are born with determine how our brains develop and that in turn how our brains develop determines how we interact with the world. Recent brain research

challenges these assumptions. Neuroscientists have found that throughout the entire process of development, beginning even before birth, the brain is affected by environmental conditions, including the kind of nourishment, care, surroundings, and stimulation an individual receives."

Wellesley, B. and J. Clark (2000)

In terms of the environment, we know a great deal about how it affects early growth and development. Studies of prenatal development point out the damage done by alcohol and chemical consumption during pregnancy. We know that in order to thrive in the early years, children need proper diet and rest. They need love, stability, security, and self-esteem. They also need sensory stimulation and human interaction. When children are the victims of poverty and poor parenting, they miss out on many if not all of these critical ingredients for having a positive start in life.

What remains troubling is that while all of these initiatives and reports argue for high quality programs and experiences for young children, there is rarely a mention of play. Yet as Vygotsky claims, play is the premier way children learn. Of all the activities of childhood none is more crucial for healthy growth and development than play. Play provides the sensory stimulation that creates the biological pathways of learning. Play shapes social interaction and generates communication. Play enables children to explore feelings and give voice to imagination. The active nature of play contributes substantially to physical development and good health. When provided with the right play environment, that is, one rich in experiences and enthusiastic play partners, then exploratory play, pretend play, and games with rules will go a long way toward ensuring a good beginning for our children.

In the absence of acknowledging play as a central piece in providing a quality life for young children, the risk of imposing developmentally inappropriate experiences and expectations on children is high. We must remember that the goal of high quality programs and experiences is the healthy all-around development of the child. It is not primarily getting ready for school. It is not to produce human capital. The goal is always the child's welfare: his fair opportunity to grow into a productive human being and the physical and mental stability that will ensure that he becomes a stable, contributing member of society according to his potential ability.

Although the most valuable years of development and learning may have passed by the time a child starts school, there is much we can do to provide optimum experiences for learning. This is particularly important given that children are starting school at an increasingly younger age with more and more children attending a full-day school program.

What Can We Do Together?

Providing the best possible start in life for our children is a heavy responsibility, primarily for parents. They need the support of teachers of young children, caregivers, and the early childhood community at large. While there is no doubt that support should be provided by governments, the good news is that there is a great deal we can do together to support our children and their learning through play.

The learning that comes from play is natural, that is, all children, no matter what culture or background, can learn the same important lessons through play. We know, however, that the kind and quality of the play experiences can make a huge difference to the kind and quality of brain development and learning.

> ➢ Work together as partners for the child's welfare. Creating real working partnerships is no easy matter, but it can be done and, for the well-being of our children, it is worth the effort. All we need is the will and the commitment to sit down openly together and pool our respective strengths and knowledge. No one knows a child better than her parents. Teachers by virtue of their professional education bring knowledge and skills that parents can find helpful. Caregivers bring observations and knowledge about a particular child that can be essential for providing a bridge between home and school.

Chart 15.1

Play in School **Junior Kindergarten, Senior Kindergarten, Grade One** **To Do List** **For Optimum Learning and Development**
Insist that no matter what the other demands, play comes first. Ideally, play will take over most of the child's time in preschool and kindergarten. In the primary grades, a *minimum* of 1 hour of uninterrupted time per half day should be protected for self-directed play.
Allow children freedom within a prepared environment. Keep rules to a minimum but set up a clear set of expectations. Freedom is only freedom when it respects the rights of all the individuals in the community of play. Otherwise we are left with self-centered bullying.
Allow for differences in developmental pace. Remember that each child has a timetable of development and there will be a considerable difference from one to another in how they act and understand.
Allow for differences in experience. Children in any setting are likely to vary greatly in their background experiences. Given that learning is closely linked to experience, it is important to know what kinds of things the child knows from experience.
Allow for differences in age. Put forth a case for play and the necessary budget to provide quality toys and materials.
Get administration on side. We cannot expect that administrators will have the knowledge to appreciate the importance of play so it is up to the teachers who are the specialists to set out a convincing rationale. One of the best ways I have found to get a principal or supervisory officer on side is to invite them to join in play with the children.
Be professional. If you have not had an opportunity to obtain professional training then build on your experiences by observing in exemplary facilities, reading, and talking to professionals. Consider taking a course or, if not available in your community, approach community planners or perhaps a local college to offer courses on play and development.

> ➢ Establish play centers in preschools and schools where parents can find information about play as well as a toy lending library. Similar to the Literature for Life Program mentioned in chapter 12, a play group can show the joy and enthusiasm for learning that comes about through play in a

place where there is sufficient space, a rich selection of toys and materials, routines, and rules that do not interfere with learning but provide safety and harmony. Play centers can provide modeling for how to play with your children. Some parents might come from a culture where play is not valued and may have little idea how to support learning through play. They may be afraid and need reassurance that whatever they feel comfortable in doing is fine.

➤ Look to Family Centers for information and examples for good parenting. These centers can offer information regarding public health and social services in the community as well as support for special needs children. They can be meeting places for parents who share a similar language and culture.

➤ Try to make your child's day as seamless as possible. It is very difficult for many parents to avoid placing their children in several settings in one day. A five-year-old child may be juggled between home, a half-day kindergarten, a childcare facility, and a baby-sitter, all in the same day. Even when each of these placements is well run, the number of different situations and sets of demands on a child causes stress. Given costs and the lack of childcare facilities in some regions, it may not be possible to avoid having your child in several settings in one day. It is important, however, to understand what this means for your child and try to minimize the stress by choosing places where the expectations and approach to child rearing are consistent with your own.

➤ Become an advocate for children's issue. In countless reports from around the globe, we find recommendations for sweeping changes in the way we deal with young children and families. Get involved in the establishment one of these community-based initiatives.

Looking Forward

I believe that perhaps the biggest barrier to implementing genuine change in early care and education is a matter of teacher education. Early education is not baby-sitting. It requires the brightest and the most talented of teachers. In most countries, preparing teachers for preschool and for school is done through different institutions with distinct curricula.

For more information on teacher qualifications in the United States see U.S. Department of Labor, www.bls.gov.

For information regarding proposed innovation in teacher education see Maxwell, Kelly. 2006. Early Childhood Teacher Preparation in the United States A National Report. *FDG Child Development Institute, the University of North Carolina at Chapel Hill.*

The biggest difference between the teacher education programs for early childhood and elementary teaching has been thought to lie in the fact that the Early Childhood Education certification programs did not have sufficient emphasis on theory, while the elementary school programs were believed to lack sufficient practical experience. These are false assumptions, and anyone who has been involved in both knows that theory and practice are central to both educational institutions (Eden and Houston 1998).

If the early years are to be taken seriously, then we need to have staff that is thoroughly trained in the theory and practice of early development and learning. It has been my personal experience that teaching in junior and senior kindergarten is the most sophisticated teaching in the entire school system. A junior kindergarten teacher does not open a textbook and assign students a formula to memorize. She is constantly making decisions based on knowledge of child development, play, the arts, and every other subject, as well as the individual needs of each child. This is teaching at its best. Giving our children anything less is shortchanging our future.

Understanding the nature of play and its role in development is not widely included in teacher education programs. In early childhood programs, there are differences in the way the study of play is conducted. In some programs play is seen as a valuable learning experience. Preoccupation with the need to appear sufficiently academic, however, has led to a phenomenon called directed play. The very word "directed" removes the spontaneity from play and reduces its effectiveness in terms of learning. How can we hope to make play central to a quality program if those delivering the program have insufficient knowledge and skill to properly implement a program?

What is needed is an early-years education degree program that combines the best of both the ECE program and the bachelor of education program. Such a program would emphasize the new understandings of child development, including the research on the development of the brain. It would emphasize health and physical well-being and the arts. It would have play as a cornerstone.

An early years degree program would include the opportunity to develop skills in partnering with parents and other members of the early childhood community. Home visits and team teaching with other ECE-trained staff would open the door for greater collaboration for those entrusted with the care and education of our young children.

In addition to the early-years degree program, there must be different levels of qualifications that allow those unable or uninterested in pursuing a degree to participate fully in the care and education of the young. There is a valuable role for assistants, artists, and other specialists to work in partnership with teachers. It's difficult to avoid a hierarchical relationship with differentiated qualifications, but it can be done. What an exciting prospect that parents, early childhood and school teachers, along with other experts might one day work in true partnership to provide the highest quality environment for our young children!

Politicians and educational administrators use slick slogans to suggest that they care about young children, but the reality sends a different message. Can there really be a place where "no child is left behind"? Can we believe that "better beginnings" for all children will include the poor, the disenfranchised, and the homeless? Is the political and societal will there to recognize that for every dollar invested in a young child, the return is manifold in adult life? We have only to examine budget allocations and broken promises to see how little difference all of the many commissions and reports of the past decades have made.

Can we make a difference, you and I? We do not have a choice. We cannot accept the decisions of bureaucrats as an excuse for inferior practices. There is too much at stake. It is not good enough that down the road in some more enlightened times we may see real improvement to the status quo. Our children depend on us to keep them safe from harm. How can we neglect to act against educational practices that undermine the spirit and joy of childhood? How can we not take up the challenge of making a difference in the way early experiences are delivered today? It is time to return play as a way of learning for all children.

Looking Forward!

Part 4
Resources and References

Resources

Recommended Toys and Activities for Play

Putting Together a Dress-up Box

Early Reading Activities

Games and Activities for Math

Recipes for Play Dough

Suggestions for Handmade Musical Instruments

Toys and Activities that Develop the Body and the Mind

While it is true that a child may play with the same toy at different ages and stages of development, he is likely to be practicing different skills appropriate to his stage. The following information is simply a guide to help parents understand the benefits of some traditional toys and activities as well as the most likely time when he will use these toys.

Toys and Play Activities that Develop the Body

1–9 months

Toys

- that rattle and/or have moving parts
- that feel good—are soft, warm, and textured such as fur or silk
- that can be cuddled, such as stuffed dolls and toys
- that can be squeezed, such as bath toys
- that encourage movement of whole body, such as crib exercisers

Games and activities

- Play pat-a-cake, peekaboo and other old favorites.
- Make funny faces and interesting sounds to encourage imitation.
- Bounce baby while holding him in a standing position.
- Place toys out of reach and encourage infant to get them.

9–18 months

Toys

- push/pull toys that encourage walking
- stacking and nesting toys

- large blocks of different shapes, sizes, and materials (wood, foam, etc.)
- large, soft balls

Games and activities

- dancing and moving to children's records or other lively music
- classic folk games such as ring-around-the-rosy
- having baby throw a big ball (he cannot yet catch it)

18 months–3 years

Toys for large motor development

- blocks of different sizes and shapes
- bats and balls in sizes suitable to the age
- pull and push toys
- indoor/outdoor ride-on toys without pedals
- rocking toys with handles for support

Toys for fine motor development

- jigsaw puzzles with large pieces
- tools such as spoons and other kitchen items
- stacking and nesting toys
- large beads and laces

Games and activities

- daily physical activity both indoors and outdoors

3–6 years

Toys for large motor development

- climbers, balance beams, and other playground equipment
- ride-on toys with pedals
- climbers, slides, and teeter-totter

Toys for fine motor development

- markers and scissors
- hammers and other construction tools
- interlocking blocks
- form boards and puzzle

Games and activities

- daily physical activity using a variety of equipment and games

Toys and Games that Develop the Mind

1–9 months

Toys

- mobiles, rattles, music-making toys, and other toys that stimulate the senses
- colorful stuffed toys
- bathtub toys
- stacking toys with a clear distinction between each part
- crib activity sets that provides many of the above experiences

Games and activities

- action games such as hide-and-seek
- rocking games
- games that use spatial concepts (over, under, behind)

9–18 months

Toys

- large, soft blocks of different geometric shapes
- sound-making toys

Games and activities

- pretend games such as "This Little Piggy"
- movement games that use spatial words, such as putting actions to the nursery rhyme "Jack and Jill"
- free play with sand, water, mud, and other materials

18 months–3 years

Toys

- jigsaw puzzles and form boards
- stacking toys (pieces stacked according to size)
- nesting toys (pieces fit inside one another)
- pattern-making toys such as beads and blocks
- dress-up clothes—purses, hats, shoes, etc.
- household items for pretend play
- toys for water play
- construction toys

Games and activities

- games that require following simple directions such as "Simon says"
- free play with natural materials

3–5 years

Toys

- manipulative toys for sorting and classifying according to color, shape, and size
- manipulative objects for sorting and classifying, such as a collection of dinosaurs, fruits and vegetables, cars and other vehicles, and buttons.
- form boards and puzzles that require visual discrimination
- interlocking blocks and construction toys
- found materials such as stones, ribbon, and lengths of cloth

Games and activities

- board games
- action songs and simple dances (bingo)
- card games, such as lotto, matching, and visual memory games

Putting Together a Dress-Up Box

What You'll Need

- a storage container such as a large box or perhaps a laundry basket in which to store costumes and props
- if there is room, a portable clothes rack or a small movable coat rack on which to hang up clothes.
- stackable storage containers for stowing props
- storage containers for materials that might be needed to make a prop: cloth, fabric glue, sequins, felt pieces, soft wire, buttons, scissors.

Basic Costumes and Props

- adult clothing that is no longer in use: women's blouses, sweaters, dresses, skirts, party clothing
- hats of all types: straw hats, sun hats, baseball caps, bonnets, whatever you can find
- shoes of all types: women's high-heeled (a must), slippers, sandals, men's footwear

Accessories

- jewelry, old watches, bracelets, eyeglasses without the glass, goggles, gloves, scarves, and purses
- men's shirts, ties, shorts, vests, fedoras, caps, helmets

To add interest

Children will improvise using the basic clothing when they play a character outside the family. To nudge them toward community themes, add such things as apron and baker's hat, firefighter's hat, doctor's bag, toy stethoscope, cell phone, postman's bag, and so on.

Taking Care of the Dress-up Box

Teach your children several basic rules for taking care of the dress-up box: Use the storage container to keep all the items together.

Things to Remember

- Ask your family and friends to donate items they no longer use.
- Check out charity shops and discount stores for interesting props and costumes.
- Don't have too much stuff out at once. The children will focus more on the props and costumes than on the pretend play.
- When you first put out the dress-up box, the children will try everything on, sometimes all at once. As they sort out what is there, they will begin to use the items as resources for their pretend play.
- If space is limited, the dress-up box can be stowed under the bed or somewhere that the children can easily pull it out when they want to play.

Experiences with Literacy in Everyday Life

Before a child can read words independently, he needs many experiences with reading in everyday life. This helps children connect signs and symbols with meaning. The following activities provide examples of what can be done.

What Does It Say?

Take your child for a walk around the block, to a park, mall, or other area in the neighborhood that displays building and business names, traffic signs, and so on.

Ask him: What do you think that word/sign says?
Why do you think that? Sample: Royal Bank

Your child might be familiar with the bank from accompanying you and would then associate this experience with the name and logo displayed on the building.

What do you think this sign tells the drivers to do?

Point to various traffic signs and have them predict. Some such as STOP may be familiar from riding on a bus or car. Other he may not have noticed before but is able to predict from the sign itself, such as the No Parking sign.

How many words can you find that start with the same letter as your name?

Look on storefronts, advertisements, and other labels and signs.

How many places can you find that have the same number on them as your age?

Look on mailboxes, house fronts, license plates, and so on.

If you could make a sign to remind people of something, what would it be?

Samples might be No Littering or Watch Out for Pets

Pantry Puzzle

Place a collection of cans and packages in a laundry basket. Have your child find all the containers that hold food that starts with the same letter.

Sample: pork and beans, pears, peaches, pumpkin, and so on

On another day, have your child sort them in a different way.

Sample: Sort into big containers and small containers.
Find all the soup cans.
Find all the cereal boxes.

Use these props to make a store.

Add play money and signs.

Puppets

A selection of puppets either commercially made or handmade encourages children to role-play. With a bit of help the children can make several simple styles of puppets. This does not mean doing a model they can copy but helping them with the technical aspects, such as cutting and pasting.

Stick Puppets

Provide circles of stiff cardboard or paper plates.
Have children design faces and add other features, such as a bow tie, a collar, or buttons.
Have children paste sticks to the back of the plate. (Throwaway chopsticks from a Chinese restaurant make an excellent sturdy stick.)

Finger Puppets

The basic pattern can be used to create people, animals, a ghost—anything a child might want to create.
Cut out a pattern from paper for a square large enough to go around a child's finger with sufficient overlap to glue it into a tube.
Children can glue on the face of a favorite character or create an original one by adding facial features.
The puppets can be made from cloth or paper.

Hand Puppets

One of the easiest hand puppets is the sock puppet.
Simply take a discarded sock and add features. It can become a dragon, a mouse, or even a person, depending on what the child wants.

Remember

Don't make samples for the children to copy.

Teach them the techniques of cutting and gluing and adding imaginative features to make the puppet their own.

There are many beautiful hand puppets on the market, and parents might consider this as a birthday gift.

Games and Activities for Math

Puzzles

What you'll need

Sheets of heavy paper, cardboard, or Bristol board
Drawings of simple objects such as fruits, vegetables, animals, dinosaurs, and so on. A good source for these drawings is coloring books.

Form board puzzles

Prepare a set of five objects such as fruits.
Trace each object onto a "games board" large enough to hold all five.
Children match each cut-out to the corresponding shape on the board.

Match-up puzzles

Trace a large picture of an object such as an apple onto three backgrounds of the same size. (Shirt cardboards are an ideal size and weight for these puzzles)
Cut one picture in half.
Cut one into thirds.
Cut one into quarters.
Children put the pieces back together.

Card Games

What you'll need

Blank playing cards
Stickers or freehand drawings

Regular playing cards

Lotto

Prepare a set of six matching pairs.
Lotto is usually played alone.
Cards are placed face down in front of the child. She turns one up, and then searches for the other matching card.
With children under age five, limit the number of pairs, but as children get good at this game, add additional pairs.

Concentration

Similar to lotto, but two children are needed for this game.
Cards are placed face down.
Child selects two cards. If they match, she takes another turn. If they don't match, she returns the cards face down, and the turn passes to her partner. The child who makes the most pairs is the winner.

Fish

Two or more children play this game.
This game is usually played with two regular deck of cards. For younger children, limit the number of pairs rather than using the entire deck.
Cards are shuffled, and each player gets one card. A third card is turned up. If one of the children can make a match, he does so and takes another turn. If there is no match, the turned-up card is placed on the bottom of the deck and another turned up. Children play until all pairs are found. The winner is the player with the most pairs.

Remember

Until around age five, children generally don't do well with turn taking. For the three- to five-year-olds, limit the number of pairs used and keep the pictures simple. Challenges can be added as children are ready by adding additional pairs and more complicated pieces for matching.

Recipes for Art Materials

Starch-Based Finger Paint

Any number of substances can be used for finger painting, including pudding mix and hand lotion. For an inexpensive medium try the following recipe:

Mix: 1 cup starch
       2 cups boiling water
       food coloring

Stir vigorously until it becomes thick and glossy.
If this doesn't happen, the water was not hot enough. Just place it on the stove and bring to a boil. You may want to add something for texture, such as sand or clear gelatin powder.
Give to the children while still warm.
This mixture will keep in the refrigerator for about 1 week.

Make-It-Yourself Play Dough

There are several recipes for play dough and a self-hardening play dough that I call Almost-Real Clay. Play dough does not harden and can be used in place of Plasticene. If it requires cooking, children may help only with supervision. These doughs provide a forgiving way to learn about sculpting without using costly modeling clay. They are reusable and mistakes can be easily repaired.

Cooked Play Dough

1 cup flour
½ cup salt
2 tbsp cream of tartar
1 cup water
2 tbsp cooking oil
few drops of food coloring

Combine flour, salt, and cream of tartar in the top of a double boiler. Add water, cooking oil, and food coloring. Mix thoroughly and cook until the mixture is no longer sticky and begins to form a lump (approximately 5 minutes). Keep play dough in a covered container, but do not refrigerate.

Uncooked Play Dough

2 cups flour
1 cup salt
1 tablespoon cooking oil
1 cup water

powder paint or food coloring mixed with small amount of water
Mix the paint with the flour and salt. Add oil and water and knead until no longer sticky.
Children enjoy the kneading of the dough and can make a wide variety of "foods" by rolling it our and using cookie cutters.
Store in a plastic zippered bag and refrigerate. It should last about 1 week. If it becomes crumbly, add a bit of water and reknead.
Small items of this dough can be baked in a 350° oven for 45 minutes

Almost-Real Clay

This clay is excellent for making small items that children can paint and decorate. It hardens white over several days and need not be baked.

2 cups baking soda
1 cup cornstarch
1 cup cold water, or enough to make a creamy mixture

Combine all ingredients in a large saucepan. Boil the mixture for about 1 minute over medium heat. When the mixture looks like wet mashed potatoes, take it off the heat. Put it on a plate and cover with a damp towel. Let it cool for 1 hour. The clay should then be ready to mold.

Here are some hints for using almost-real clay.

- This clay can either be shaped by hand or cut with a knife.

- If the clay begins to feel crumbly or cracks, knead it with wet hands.
- Objects that are too thin will crack when dry.
- If the object is too thick, it may crumble when dried.
- To make beads or ornaments, cut a paper pattern first, then trace it onto the clay with a toothpick and cut the shape with a small knife.
- To make hanging objects, use a toothpick to make a hole near the top, taking care not to go too close to the edge.
- Press all decorations firmly into the clay while it is wet.
- Put finished objects on a tray where they won't be disturbed, and leave them for several days to a week. After just one day, they may look hard, but they are likely to be wet inside.
- When dry, objects can be painted.

Some simple preparations can make finger painting enjoyable for everyone:

- Cover the painting surface with a large piece of plastic, such as a summer tablecloth or oilcloth, available at fabric stores.
- Provide cover-ups, such as an old shirt with sleeves cut off.
- Have a basin of soapy water and towel available right at the paint station for clean up.
- Teach children to clean up the paint station when finished. If allowed to dry, the paint can be harder to remove.
- Choose paper that is heavy enough to withstand the pressure of the hands and the moisture from the paint.

If you dampen the surface of the table, the paper will not slip. You may also tape the paper down at the corners to provide a firm base for finger painting.

Ideas for Handmade Musical Instruments

For very young children, the teacher will make these instruments but when children are old enough they provide a great project for children.

Things You'll Need

Lengths of doweling (approximately 12 [30cm] long and ¾ inch [2–3 cm] thick).
Plastic bottles with lids—various sizes
Empty tin cans—various sizes
Metal Christmas bells
Dried rice, corn, and metallic pieces
Paint
Clear enamel paint or shellac
Masking or duct tape
Scissors
Materials for decorating

Rhythm Sticks

Have local hardware store cut doweling into 12" lengths.
Sandpaper the ends to make them smooth.
Paint them bright colors.
When dry, cover them with a coat of clear enamel.
Children keep time to music by hitting two sticks together.

Shaker in a Bottle

You need to experiment to find which dry items make the most pleasing sound and also how much to add to each container. You can actually make quite a nice collection of various sounds by using different materials and different quantities.
Decorate the bottles with various kinds of paper and glue.

Drum

Remove the lid from a large juice can. Clean the can and make sure that the edge is smooth.

Using a saucepan lid bigger than the top of the can, cut out about six circles from heavy brown paper. Cover the can with a circle, press down over the sides, and fasten down tightly with tape. Repeat this step until you have a firm surface of six to eight circles. You can decorate the can with paint or cover it with paper and make a collage.

These instruments make a great addition to your prop box.

References

Ashton-Warner, Sylvia. 1963. *Teacher*. New York: Simon & Schuster.

Bergen, Doris. 1998. Stages of play development. In *Readings From Play as a Medium for Learning and Development*. Ed. D. Bergen. Olney, MD: Association for Childhood Education International.

Booth, David, and Bill Moore. 1988. *Poems please: Sharing poetry with children*. Markham, ON: Pembroke Publishers.

Boyd, B. J. 1997. Teacher response to superhero play: To ban or not to ban. *Childhood Education*, 74 (1): 23–28.

Calkins, L. M. 1986. *The art of teaching writing*. Portsmouth, NH: Heinemann.

Cambourne, Brian. 1988. *The whole story: Natural learning and the acquisition of language in the classroom*. Aukland, New Zealand: Ashton Scholastic Limited.

Carson, Rachel. 1984. *The sense of wonder*. New York: Harper and Row.

Chilton-Pearce, J. 1977. *The magical child*. New York: E.P. Dutton.

Cohen, Lawrence J. 2001. *Playful parenting*. New York: Ballantyne Books.

Courtney, Richard. 1982. *Re-Play*. Toronto, ON: OISE Press.

David, Paulo. 2006. Commentary on the United Nations Convention of the Rights of the Child, Article 31: The Right to Leisure, Play and Culture.

Eden, Susanne, and Brenda Grandinetti. 1994. Capes, crowns and a three-bean salad: Play and literacy in kindergarten. *Canadian Children*, Spring, Vol. A, No. 1.

Eden, Susanne, and Marilee Houston. 1998. *The practicum: A shared context for professional development of host teachers and student teachers in early childhood and faculty of education preservice.* Unpublished report. Toronto: York University

Eisner, Eliot. 1990. The role of art and play in children's cognitive development. In *Children's Play and Learning: Perspectives and Policy Implications.* Ed. Edgar W. Klugman and Sara Smilansky. New York: Teachers College Press.

Erikson, E. 1976. *Toys and reasons.* New York: W. W. Norton.

Ferguson, Marilyn. 1987. *The Aquarian conspiracy: Personal and social transformation in our time.* Los Angeles: J. P. Tarcher.

Friendly, Martha, Jane Beach, Carolyn Ferns and Michele Turiano. 2006. Early childhood education in Canada 2006. 7th edition. Toronto, On: Childcare Resource and Research.

Froebel, F. 1898. *The education of man.* New York: Appleton.

Frost, J. L. 1992. *Play and playscapes.* Albany NY: Delmar.

Frost, J. L., and Sylvia Sunderlin. 1985. When children play. In *Proceedings of the International Conference on Play and Play Environments.* Wheaton, MD: Association for Childhood Education International.

Gallahue, D. 1976. *Motor development and movement experiences for young children.* Toronto, ON: John Wiley & Sons.

Gardner, Howard. 1994. *The arts and human development.* New York: Basic Books.

Goodman. Kenneth. 1968. The psycholinguistic nature of the reading process. In *The psycholinguistic nature of the reading process*. Ed. Kenneth Goodman. Detroit, MI: Wayne State University Press.

Gordon, Andrea. 2007. "Simple Fun." *Toronto Star*. November 24, 2007.

Government of Victoria, Australia, Department of Human Services. 2007. *Best Start: Project Overview*. www.BestStart@dhs.vic.gov. au.

Graves, D. 1983. *Writing: Teachers and children at work*. Portsmouth, NH: Heinemann.

Gronlund, Gaye. 1992. Coping with ninja turtle play in my kindergarten classroom. *Young Children*, 48.

Heckman, James J. 2005. Cited in *What do we know about early learning and what are we doing about it?* Fraser Mustard. Early Childhood Development - Public Policy Conference Address to the Canadian Educational Association.

Heckman, James J. 2007. *Emerging economic arguments for investing in the health of our children's learning*. An interview with Dr. Heckman by Children of the Code Series. www.childrenofthecode. org.

Henninger, Michael. 1985. Preschool children's play behaviors in an indoor and outdoor environment. In *When Children Play: Proceedings of the International Conference on Play and Play Environments*. Ed. J. L. Frost and Sylvia Sunderlin. Wheaton, MD: Association for Childhood Education International.

Hertzman. Clyde. 2002. *Forward to BC early childhood development action plan: A work in progress*. Victoria, BC: Government of British Columbia.

Hirsch, E., ed. 1984. *The block book*. Rev. ed. Washington, DC: National Association for the Education of Young Children.

Jarrold, C., J. Boucher, and P. K. Smith. 1996. Generalitivity deficits in pretend play in autism. *British Journal of Developmental Psychology*, 14.

Johnson, James, James Christie, and Thomas Yawkey. 1987. *Play and early childhood development*. Harper Collins Publisher.

Jones, Gerald 2002. *Killing monsters: Why children need fantasy, superheroes, and make-believe violence*. New York: Basic Books.

Kamii, Constance. 1985. *Young children reinvent arithmetic: Implications of Piaget's theory*. New York: Teachers College Press.

Kamii, Constance. *Autonomy: the aim of education envisioned by Piaget*. Published in Phi Delta Kappen date unknown.

Kotulak, Richard. 1996. Inside the Brain. Cited in The brain and early childhood, facilitaor's guide. ASCD, Alexandria: Virginia.

Levin, Diane E. 1998. *Remote control childhood? Combating the hazards of media culture*. Washington, DC: NAEYC.

Magnusdottir, Sigridur Ruth. 1996. *Socio-dramatic play: A context for the negotiation of conflict*. Unpublished master's of education thesis. York University, Faculty of Education. Toronto, ON.

Masse, Louise, and Richard Tremblay. 1997. *Behavior of boys in kindergarten and the onset of substance use during adolescence*. Canadian Institute for Advanced Research. University of British Columbia, Vancouver, B.C. Canada

Maxwell, Kelly. 2006. *Early childhood teacher preparation program in the United States: A national report*. The University of North Carolina at Chapel Hill: FPG Child Development Institute.

McCain, M. N. and J. Fraser Mustard. 1999. *Early years study. Final report: Reversing the real brain drain.* Toronto: Publications Ontario.

McQuay-Sellwood, Dianne. 1998. *The nature of superhero play in kindergarten.* Unpublished master's of education thesis. York University, Faculty of Education. Toronto, ON.

Moffitt, Mary. 1984. Children learn science through block play. In *The block book.* Rev. edition. Ed. E. Hirsch. Washington, DC: NAEYC

Mustard, J. Fraser. 2005. *What do we know about early learning and what are we doing about it?* Early Childhood Development - Public Policy Conference Address to the Canadian Educational Association.

Odam, S. L., S. R. McConnell, and L. K. Chandler. 1993. Acceptability and feasibility of classroom-based social interaction interventions for young children with disabilities. *Exceptional Children,* 60 (3).

Organization for Economic Cooperation and Development. 2006. *Starting strong II: Early childhood education and care.*

Orr, David W. 1992. *Ecological literacy: Education and the transition to a postmodern world.* Albany, NY: State University of New York Press.

Ontario Ministry of Education. 1983. *Report of the Junior Kindergarten, Kindergarten, Grade One Task Force.* Ontario Government Publication.

Parten, M. 1933. Social participation among pre-school children. *Journal of Abnormal and Social Psychology.*

Piaget, Jean and B. Inhelder. 1969. The psychology of the child. New York: Basic Books

Pica, Rae. 2003. *Your active child*. New York: MacGraw Hill.

Rivkin, Mary. 1995. *The great outdoors: Restoring children's right to play outside*. Washington, DC: NAEYC.

Rubin, K. H., and R. J. Coplan. 1998. Social and nonsocial play in childhood: An individual differences perspective. In *Multiple perspectives on play in early childhood*. Ed. O. N. Saracho and B. Spodek. Albany: State University of New York Press.

Scarfe, Neville. 1990. *The Scarfe papers*. Vancouver, BC: The Children's Play Resource Centre.

Singer, Dorothy, and Jerome Singer. 1992. *The house of make-believe*. Cambridge, MA: Harvard University Press.

Singer, Dorothy, and Jerome Singer, 2000. *Make-believe: Games and activities for imaginative play*. Washington, DC: Magination Press.

Smilansky, Sara. 1990. Socio-dramatic play: Its relevance to behavior and achievement in school. In *Children's play and learning: Perspectives and policy implications*. Ed. Edgar W. Klugman and Sara Smilansky. New York: Teachers College Press.

Smith, Frank. 1983. *Essays into literacy*. London: Exeter Heinemann Educational Books.

Statistics Canada and Human Resources Development Canada. 1995)*National longitudinal survey of children: Overview of survey instruments for 1994-1995*. Statistics Canada Catalogue. Ministry of Industry. Ottawa, ON.

Talbot, Margaret. 2006. "The Baby Lab." *New Yorker*. September 4.

Tremblay, Ernest Richie. 1998. *How constructive block play supports the development of literacy in kindergarten*. Unpublished master's of education thesis. York University, Faculty of Education. Toronto, ON.

Tremblay, M. S., and J. D. Willms. 2003. Is the Canadian childhood obesity epidemic related to physical inactivity. *International Journal of Obesity*, 27 (9).

Tremblay, Richard E., Jaana Haapasalo, and Louise Masse. 1994. *Can physically aggressive boys survive in school?* Canadian Institute for Advanced Research.

Turnbull, Barbara. 2005. "The Word in Hope." *Toronto Daily Star.* September 5.

U.S. National Institutes of Health. 1998. *Clinical guidelines for identification, evaluation and treatment of overweight and obesity in adults.* Bethesda, MD: National Institutes of Health.

Vanderwater, Elizabeth, Mi-Suk Shim, and Allison Caplovitz. 2004. Linking obesity and activity levels with children's television and video game use. *Journal of Adolescence*, 27 (1).

Vygotsky, Lev. 1962. *Thought and language.* Cambridge, MA: MIT Press.

Vygotsky, Lev. 1976. Play: Its role in the mental development of the child. In *Play: Its role in development.* Ed. J. Bruner et al. New York: Basic Books.

Wasserman, Selma, and George Ivany. 1988. *Teaching elementary science: Who's afraid of spiders?* New York: Harper and Row.

Wasserman, Selma. 1990. *Serious players in the primary classroom.* New York: Teachers College Press, Columbia University.

Wheatley, M., and M. Kellner-Rogers. 1996. *A simpler way.* San Francisco: Berret-Koehler.

Weininger, Otto. 1982. *Out of the minds of babes.* Chicago. Illinois: Chas. Thomas Publications.

White, Randy, and Vicki Stoecklin. 1998. *Children's outdoor play & learning environments: Returning to nature.* Kansas City, MO: White Hutchinson Leisure and Learning Group.

Yardley, Alice. 1970. *Senses and sensitivity.* London: Evans Bros.

Yardley, Alice. 1973. *Young children thinking.* London: Evans Bros.

Bibliography of Children's Literature

There are so many wonderful books for children that I could not attempt to provide a comprehensive bibliography. The books listed below are ones that have been mentioned in this book or have been favorites of the children in my world. For those wishing to start a library of children's literature, these make a good beginning.

Patterned Text and Predictable Books

Mother Goose

Lobel, Arnold. 1986. *The just right Mother Goose*. New York: Random House.

Miranda, Anne, and Janet Stevens. 1987. *To market to market*. New York: Harcourt Brace.

Opie, Iona. 1996. *My very first Mother Goose*. Cambridge, MA: Candlewick.

Oxenbury, Helen. 2004. *The Helen Oxenbury nursery collection*. New York: Alfred A Knopf.

Wildsmith, Brian. 1964. *Brian Wildsmith's Mother Goose*. New York: Franklin Watts.

Alphabet books

Cleaver, Beverly. 1982. *ABC*. Toronto, ON: Kids Can Press.

Edwards, Wallace. 2002. *Alphabeasts*. Toronto, ON: Kids Can Press.

Lear, Edward. 1983. *An Edward Lear alphabet*. New York: Lithrop, Lee & Shepard Books.

Pallotta, Jerry. 1986. *The icky bug alphabet book*. New York: Scholastic.

Viorst, Judith. 1994. *The alphabet from Z to A*. New York: Atheneum.

Counting Books

Addshead, Paul. 1995. *One odd old owl*. New York: Child's Play.

Gustafson, Scott. 1995. *Animal orchestra: A counting book*. New York: Greenwich.

Fleming, Denise. 1992. *Count*. New York: Scholastic.

Pallotta, Jerry. 1992. *The icky bug counting book*. Watertown, MA: Charlesbridge.

Cumulative Tales

Hawkins, C. and J. Hawkins. 1987. *I know an old lady who swallowed a fly*. New York: Putman.

Ardema, Verna. 1981. *Bringing the rain to Kapiti Plain*. New York: Dial Books.

Picture Books Without Text

Mayer, Mercer. 1969. *Frog, where are you*. New York: Dial Books

Popov, Nikolai. 1995. *Why?* New York: North-South Books.

Picture Books New and Old

Brown, Margaret Wise. 1947. *Goodnight moon.* New York: Harper and Row.

Brown, Margaret Wise. 1975. *Goodnight moon room: A pop-up book.* New York: Harper and Row.

Carle, Eric. 1969. *The very hungry caterpillar.* New York: Philomel.

Carle, Eric. 1977. *The grouchy ladybug.* New York: HarperCollins.

Cherry, Lynne. 1988. *Who's sick today?* New York: EP Dutton.

Curtis, Jamie Lee. 1996. *Tell me again about the night I was born.* Markham, ON: Scholastic.

Falconer, Ian. 2000. *Olivia.* New York: Athenium Books.

Keats, J. Ezra. 1976. *The snowy day.* New York: Puffin Books.

Kovalski, Maryanne. 1987. *The wheels on the bus.* London: Little Brown.

Krauss, Ruth and Maurice Sendak. 2005. *Bears.* Harper Collins.

Lear, Edward. 1984. *The owl and the pussy cat.* New York: Scholastic.

Lee, Dennis. 1974. *Alligator pie.* Toronto, ON: MacMillan.

Mayer, Mercer. 1968. *There's a nightmare in my closet.* New York: Dial.

Mayer, Mercer. 2007. *Grandma, grandpa, and me.* New York: Harper Collins.

Opie, Iona Archibald and Rosemary Wells. 2007. *Mother Goose's little treasures*. Cambridge, MA: Candlewick Press.

Rosen, M. 1989. *We're going on a bear hunt*. New York: MacMillan.

Sendak, Maurice. 1963. *Where the wild things are*. New York: Harper and Row.

Wells, Rosemary. 1997. *Bunny cakes*. New York: Scholastic.

Shannon, David. 2006. *Good boy, Fergus*. Blue Sky Press.

Straaten, Herman van. 2007. *Duck tails*. New York: North-South Books.

Umansky, Kaye, and Nick Sharratt. 1999. *Tickle my nose and other action rhymes*. London: Penguin Books.

Willems, Mo. 2003. *Don't let the pigeon drive the bus!* New York: Hyperion Books.

Willis, Jeanne, and Tony Ross. 1999. *The boy who lost his belly button*. London: Random House.

Yarrow, Peter, Lenny Lipton, and Eric Puybaret. 2007. *Puff the magic dragon*. New York: Sterling Publishing Co.

Zolotow, C. 1972. *William's doll*. New York: Harper and Row.